WAKINYAN

Lakota Religion in the Twentieth Century

STEPHEN E. FERACA

University of Nebraska Press
Lincoln and London

First Bison Books printing: 2001
Most recent printing indicated by the
last digit below:
10 9 8 7 6 5 4 3 2 1
Library of Congress Cataloging-
in-Publication Data:
Feraca, Stephen E., 1934–
Wakinyan : Lakota religion in
the twentieth century /
Stephen E. Feraca.
p. cm. Includes
bibliographical references.
ISBN 0-8032-2004-9
(cl: alk. paper)
ISBN 0-8032-6905-6
(pa: alk. paper)
1. Teton Indians—Religion.
I. Title.
E99.T34F47   1998
299'.7852—dc21
97-37893
CIP

TO ALL THE LAKOTA PEOPLE WHO
ARE GENUINELY RESPECTFUL OF THE
TRADITIONAL RELIGION, *and*
TO THOSE WHO HAVE SO KINDLY
ASSISTED THE AUTHOR FOR A PERIOD
APPROACHING HALF A CENTURY.

Wóphila tȟáka wa'ų́ na iyúha napéčiyuza.
Wačhíyąpi, lé miyé lo.

CONTENTS

ILLUSTRATIONS

PREFACE

The major part of this book was originally published in 1963 by the Museum of the Plains Indian in Browning, Montana, as number 2 in the series Studies in Plains Anthropology and History. As a publication of the Department of the Interior, Bureau of Indian Affairs, it was in the public domain for a long time. Out of print shortly after it made its appearance, it has been copied and recopied, quite legally, by many persons in this country and in Europe. I myself wearied of making copies and explaining that it was otherwise unavailable.

This work concerns traditional Lakota religion in the twentieth century, a timespan devoid of tribal buffalo hunting and other major aspects of the former nomadic, equestrian, tipi-dwelling Northern Plains culture, unmarked by warfare with other tribes and the United States Army, and entirely within a setting influenced by an administered reservation system. Traditional religion is herein treated as recognizing, respecting, acquiring, and utilizing supernatural power in terms of such beliefs and practices deriving from the pre- and early-reservation period. The title, *Wakinyan*, refers to the Thunderbird or Winged Deity of the Lakotas, a powerful manifestation of supernatural presence in human affairs.

Although religious practices are always changing, as many changed for the Lakotas as they moved toward and then established themselves on the Northern Plains, traditional religion nevertheless retains its fundamental qualities, governed by the concept of supernatural power. The belief in such power, from whatever source it may be derived, exists in itself and apart from any particular observance or activity.

In the context of the twentieth century, understanding what is traditional in Lakota religion can only be achieved with attention to each succeeding (or preceding) generation of "old-timers." The Lakotas rationalize their beliefs and rites in terms of what they think is proper in the view of the aged, whether or not the successively younger people are themselves truly aware of what transpired earlier. In this respect I have often been greatly impressed at the ease with which many Lakotas are able to make generational leaps backward, even to previous centuries, to justify what they perceive to be a traditional aspect of a given religious ceremony.

The power concept in itself I have never heard denied by a Lakota of any sociological category, including those who have no personal association with any expression of traditional religion. If such a concept does not have meaning for them, they nevertheless accept that it existed before them and was indeed powerful. Those who remain aloof from traditional religion share with those who participate in any of its many manifestations a combination of fear and respect. This combination, it can be assumed, existed aboriginally. For the Lakotas, the concepts of fear and respect are, in a religious sense, virtually indistinguishable.

What is genuinely traditional is gauged not by comparing or contrasting, for example, someone who has never tied tobacco in cloth for an offering with another who often does so, but by assessing their differing levels of respect for the power associated with such ritual. In like manner, between individuals who prepare and offer such articles, the quantity and quality of the goods are not in themselves of much value in demonstrating personal adherence to tradition. A Lakota who makes a relatively valuable sacrifice may actually possess much less of a traditional attitude than someone who has never done so. Indeed, the latter believer may have never entered into any such practice simply because of fear of not being sufficiently knowledgeable or prepared to approach the powers. Traditionalists fear not only those who abuse or misuse things religious but the power itself, a seminal element often lost in the numerous descriptions and discussions of Lakota religion.

Basically an ethnography, this work is also, I trust, humanistic in flavor and conveys some of the dynamics of traditional religion as it operates in

Lakota life. In these pages I attempt to evaluate the vitality of religious tradition in the face of the destruction of the previous century's economic base, the onslaught of a federally imposed system with its generally harmful policies and programs responsible for the continued dependence of the Lakota people, Christianization, and the myriad cultural and economic demands of the larger society.

Although religious phenomena, along with much of the rest of Lakota culture, have changed significantly since this work was first written in the early 1960s, pre- and early-reservation beliefs and practices remain very much with the people, many of whom, however, express great concern and even fear regarding increasing visibility and publicity coupled with decreasing authenticity and respect. The tenacity of traditional religion remains fascinating in view of the technological advances with which almost all Lakotas are now generally familiar. I have placed some emphasis on the influence traditional religion continues to have on the many and varied, and often tragic, problems facing the Lakotas. Along with the economy and education, the general mental and physical health of the people is firmly related to aboriginal religious concepts that influence even those who may have little or nothing to do with traditional religion per se.

In this revision of the 1963 publication, the text remains largely unaltered. Changes have been made to conform to modern usage, for clarification and stylistic purposes, and to correct a few outright errors and dispense with extraneous material, some of this accomplished by the simple expedient of deletion. Some new material has been added or appears in endnotes. The Lakota orthography has been improved and expanded.[1] A recommended bibliography has been added.

The most important alterations to the original work are not so much revisions as expansions and updates. These are primarily mandated by a review of pertinent literature, by information gathered in numerous discussions with colleagues and consultants, in brief trips to Pine Ridge since 1962, and by the results of new fieldwork in 1996. The results of that recent fieldwork will be published in a volume dealing with the state of Lakota religion at the close of the century. Some data and observations pertaining to the religious scene of the 1990s, as it evolved from the early 1960s, are found in the endnotes.

To obtain the data found in these pages, I spent various periods, usually during the summers, on the Pine Ridge Reservation, with some time during those periods devoted to work on the adjoining Rosebud Reservation. The summers of 1954 and 1955 were mainly occupied in the study of the Sun Dance. With the assistance of a small grant from Columbia University, I devoted the following year to the *yuwípi* ceremony and herbalism. In this field study I was joined by Walter Karp, a fellow graduate student from Columbia. A term during the summer of 1958 was occupied by further studies of the Sun Dance and herbalism, and I devoted the summer of 1959 to peyotism and darkened-room or night ceremonies other than *yuwípi*.

Study continued during my employment as Agency Field Representative on Pine Ridge from 1959 through 1962 and proceeds to the present with fieldwork conducted, as previously mentioned, during the summer of 1996. I focused on aged Oglála consultants, primarily concerning their views on the activities of younger people and non-Indians. Most interviews were tape-recorded. Rather informal conversations and observations of Sun Dances were, as always, invaluable.

TERMINOLOGY

The 1963 publication was subtitled "Contemporary Teton Dakota Religion," the tribal designation the result of the editor's insistence on following anthropological usage of that day. Many modern Lakota, or Teton Sioux, people, along with many non-Lakotas, reject the term *Sioux*, which is now regarded as a pejorative appellation. It derives from the French spelling of the last syllable of an Odawa (Ottawa) term for a species of rattlesnake. Throughout this work *Lakota* has, except in certain identifications, replaced the terms *Teton* and *Sioux*. Care must nevertheless be taken in employing the designation *Lakota*. In recent decades *Lakota* has all too often resembled a cliché, a factor of some significance in the study of Lakota traditional religion. In the 1990s many non-Lakota Sioux are erroneously identified as Lakotas. Some of the uninformed tend to speak of much of North American Indian religion as Lakota religion and in so doing to use Lakota terminology or the English equivalent; and an alarming number of "Plastic Indians," including Indians and non-Indians far removed from South Dakota, are calling themselves "Lakotas."

A note is in order concerning the derivation of the term *wašíčhu*, which is found throughout this account. Sioux people of all cultural and linguistic divisions have forgotten, or deny, that *wašíčhu* is an old name for a medicine or sacred bundle. It was applied to the seemingly magical bundles of trade goods transported by the first whites seen in the Great Lakes area, the French. Their guns and other metal weapons and tools, mirrors, glass beads, and cloth were *wakhą́*, that is, sacred, mysterious, and powerful. To this day, some Sioux distinguish the French from other whites by calling them *wašíčhu ikčéka*, real (or regular or original) whites.

PRONUNCIATION

The Lakota orthography used herein is as follows: "č" = "ch"; "š" = "sh"; "ǧ" is a voiced postvelar fricative (like the French "r"); "ȟ" is an unvoiced postvelar fricative (like "ch" in German *ach*); "ž" is a voiced fricative (like the "s" in *fusion*); a hook under a vowel indicates that the vowel is nasalized; "'" is a glottal stop (as in *oh-oh*); stress is indicated by an accent mark; and aspiration is indicated by "h."

ACKNOWLEDGMENTS

Very sincere appreciation is extended to James H. Howard, a longtime specialist in Plains Indian culture whose passing is greatly lamented, for his constructive criticism of the original manuscript; to the many friends who have encouraged the writing of the present work; and to the many Lakotas who contributed to my studies. In the 1996 fieldwork, made possible by a grant from the Wisconsin Humanities Council, Alexander G. Young, a graduate student in anthropology at American University, provided assistance. I owe special thanks to him and to Calvin Jumping Bull, an Oglála instructor in history and tradition who joined us in the fieldwork, and to my son Lawrence for producing the artwork.

Any researcher on the Lakota reservations must contend with the widespread belief that information regarding tradition will make an interested *wašíčhu* fabulously wealthy. However, I resided with Lakota families and individuals during much of my time on the reservations and experienced little difficulty obtaining data and advice. For example, in 1996 only two individuals, both of the "light mixed-blood" sociological category (if readers will pardon my use of this now unpopular but nevertheless representative terminology), raised the accusations of exploitation for monetary gain or of potential distortion. Most Lakotas have been extremely cooperative and candid with me over a period of more than forty years. Very few refused to discuss matters concerning religion. I am particularly anxious that the Lakota people recognize their contributions to this work and receive it kindly.

WAKINYAN

ONE

A BRIEF HISTORY OF THE LAKOTAS

It is necessary to scan pertinent aspects of the history of the Lakotas in order to begin discussing their religion. First, we must identify the tribes with which we will be concerned. This narrative concerns almost exclusively the Oglála Lakotas and Sičháǧu Lakotas (Upper Brulés) of the Pine Ridge and Rosebud Reservations, respectively. There is a tendency to speak of these people as Pine Ridge and Rosebud Sioux, thus ignoring the older tribal designations. The Sičháǧus are in fact officially known as the Rosebud Sioux Tribe, and the Oglálas as the Oglala Sioux Tribe, on the basis of their written constitutions. In referring to the Rosebud group, the term Sičháǧu and not Brulé has been chosen simply because neither they nor the neighboring Oglálas use the term Brulé, which so often appears in the literature. The term Sioux in and of itself is problematic.[1]

Upon European contact in the 1600s, the Sioux were in Minnesota and adjacent areas. The Prairie and Woodland cultures still have bearing upon contemporary Lakota religion. Shortly after meeting Europeans (mainly the French), the Sioux and the Ojibwes, Crees, and their other enemies became influenced by the fur trade and obtained guns and other weapons. With these weapons warfare intensified in the ancient dispute over territory, but already, as a result of the effects of imported disease and intertribal warfare, many Sioux were gravitating toward the northern plains and the buffalo herds (Anderson 1980; White 1978). The trek westward included the Lakotas, who generally functioned as the advance guard. Before actually leaving the prairies of western Minnesota, this division of the confederacy was identified by the name *Thíthųwą*, or Prairie Dwellers, also known as the Teton Sioux. By the end of the eighteenth century the Oglálas and Sičhą́ǧus were mounted and had pushed on as far as the true plains west of the Missouri River. Five other Lakota subdivisions, together with a split-off from the Sičhą́ǧus, were formed to the north of the Oglálas and the Sičhą́ǧus. They are now known as the Northern Tetons or Saone.[2]

The Lakotas have long since forgotten the externals of their former Prairie and Woodland cultures and, in fact, have for some time adamantly maintained that they originated in the Black Hills of South Dakota and Wyoming. This has profoundly influenced their conception of traditional culture, including religion, which most Lakotas believe derives from their origin in the Black Hills. The hills are regarded as sacred. In particular, the most prominent peaks are thought to be very sacred in themselves and ceremonies conducted on or near them conducive to the acquisition of power.

Lakota religion, however, did not suffer from the same drastic changes as other cultural elements, such as those directly related to the nomadic equestrian life like buffalo hunting and the trading of buffalo robes. The adoption of such ceremonies as the Plains Sun Dance or Medicine Lodge became a new method of approaching deities or powers previously known in Minnesota. I do not mean to imply that such tribes as the Cheyennes and Arikaras did not contribute to Lakota religion.[3] Such an implication would be false in view of the many practices acquired by the Lakotas from their neighbors. The point is that the concepts associated with spiritual power remained unchanged when the Lakotas reached and conquered the northern plains. *Wakhą́ Thą́ka* is the summation of all religious forces or powers. The Lakota religion then is synonymous with the concept of power, or *tǫ́*, as it relates to all supernatural sources. This power is never entirely controlled and is always volatile. It is, therefore, often difficult to distinguish the benevolent from the malevolent forces.

Before the mid–nineteenth century the Lakotas became dependent on traders and trading posts and began to intermarry with whites, and thus were at least introduced to Christianity. It was probably at this time that *Wakhą́ Thą́ka* began to be equated with the Christian Deity, a correspondence later reinforced by resident clergy and others at the agencies.

With the arrival of military posts in Lakota country in the 1860s to protect immigrant trains (Fort Laramie having been established earlier), a period of intense warfare began. There had been earlier hostilities involving whites, and during this period and extending well into the 1870s the Lakotas did not neglect their Indian enemies. We do not know precisely why the Lakota Sun Dance was originally conducted. It is clear, however, that during the nineteenth century it was essentially a warrior ceremony, in which the participants prayed for power to achieve success in battle and to capture horses or fulfilled vows made in thanksgiving for such success (Densmore 1918, 84–130).

The Lakotas—allied with Yanktonais and some Santee Sioux—Northern Cheyennes, and Arapahoes, with Southern Plains tribes operating in their own territory, moved Congress and then President Ulysses S. Grant to formulate a "peace policy." Treaties were made to pacify the tribes, to effect land cessions, and to create reservation boundaries within which to contain and "civilize" (also read Christianize) the warrior societies. We can only skim this period, but what is critical to the study of religion is that, with the celebrated Sioux Treaty of 1868, one of the most controversial documents in American history, the Lakotas began to live as supervised agency Indians. The Red Cloud Agency for the Oglálas and the Spotted Tail Agency for those Sičháǧus with whom we are concerned were established in the Nebraska panhandle (actually outside the South Dakota Great Sioux Reservation). At these agencies began the scrutiny of the whole of Lakota culture, including religion, by generally unsympathetic officials.

In other parts of Lakota country, and even farther west and north, the more independent groups, such as those under Sitting Bull and Crazy Horse, held out until after Custer met his defeat in 1876. Agency Lakotas periodically joined these people who resisted any outside interference. Most Lakotas had already reduced their hunting of the buffalo, were moving to and from agency headquarters to receive their rations and other goods, and found themselves under extreme pressure to sell the Black Hills. That area was not ceded or sold but actually taken from the Lakotas and the Yanktonais under an 1876 "agreement," this spurious document being incorporated in an 1877 act made in clear violation of the Treaty of 1868. There is hardly any aspect of Lakota perceptions of traditional religion that is not in some manner associated with the loss of the Black Hills.[4]

After prolonged haggling, new agencies were selected for the Oglálas and Sičhą́ǧus. In 1878, in the southwestern part of South Dakota, the Pine Ridge and Rosebud Agencies were established within the Great Sioux Reservation. The Oglálas moved to Pine Ridge and the Sičhą́ǧus to Rosebud (they became separate reservations in 1889).

Life at these agencies was not good. Custer's defeat and the war of 1876–77 had hardened Washington policy toward the Lakotas, whether they had been among the "hostiles" or not. At this time the missionaries began to make their influence felt at the agencies. Missionaries had been known to the Lakotas, but not until the creation of Pine Ridge and Rosebud did proselytizing become truly effective. Under federal policy, agencies were assigned to specific churches. The Oglálas at Pine Ridge, for example, were initially slated for the Episcopalians, but Catholic and then Presbyterian clergy made successful demands for shared access. The tolerant Lakotas, accustomed only to the native power concept and lacking what might be characterized as a proselytizing, nationalistic religion, were at first confused but eventually became influenced by the various missionaries. Thus most Lakotas learned about Christ when the buffalo were gone, when rations had been cut drastically and all efforts at farming had failed.

Another Indian in the far-off Nevada desert heard about Christ. He was Jack Wilson, better known to history as Wovoka of the Northern Paiutes. Wovoka's father was a medicine man and possibly an epileptic. Wovoka definitely was, and in 1889 his poverty-stricken people were awaiting the coming of the Messiah. Wovoka had assured them that in the near future the Messiah would appear to all Indians, since the whites had crucified him, and the buffalo and other game, together with the ghosts of the Indian dead, would return to earth. The whites would disappear. Accordingly, the Paiutes and others began to dance the newly organized Ghost Dance. The Lakotas heard about it and Short Bull and Kicking Bear, among others, went to see it for themselves (Mooney 1896).

Many of the oppressed, hungry Lakotas took up the Ghost Dance and, by the summer of 1890, were dancing the mystic, circular rite with excessive devotion. Agency officials were alarmed, but most did not expect hostilities to erupt. However, bloodshed started on 15 December 1890, with the killing of Sitting Bull, the Húkpapha Lakota chief and medicine man, on Standing Rock Reservation. As the chief resisted arrest by Indian police in the employ of agent James McLaughlin, he was shot, and word of his death spread like wildfire among the Lakotas. Word reached Pine Ridge, where a large Oglála-Sičháǧu Ghost Dance camp was situated.

During Christmas week a band of refugees, Mnikhówožus with some Húkpaphas, led by Big Foot (Spotted Elk) from Cheyenne River Reservation, was met by cavalry and directed to Wounded Knee Creek on Pine Ridge. The Lakotas encamped peaceably (they were merely seeking a safe place in which to await the Messiah and avoid police and troops) and were then ordered to surrender their guns. The massacre—it was hardly a battle—that ensued on 29 December is infamous in U.S. Army history. The cavalry, who were not expecting a fight, had nevertheless previously trained Hotchkiss guns on the encampment. Many of the casualties among the troops were unquestionably the result of what has since been termed "friendly fire." Convinced by the band's medicine man that their "ghost shirts" were indeed bulletproof, the Lakotas fearlessly faced the troops. Accounts are confused but the carnage started when a young Lakota either began firing or his rifle accidentally discharged when troopers attempted to take it (Mooney 1896, 869–70; Mattes 1960, 6). The Hotchkiss guns shredded the tipis; the shells observed no distinction between sex or age. Big Foot and many of the other dead were buried in a mass grave at the top of a hill, the location of the gun emplacement, beside which a Catholic chapel stood for many years.[5] The grave is marked with an inscribed monument erected by the survivors of the massacre. The psychological impact of this site on the Lakotas cannot be minimized.

Early in this century the land-allotment system was forced on the Lakotas. This dealt a telling blow to band organization since it provided for the allotment of the reservation land in severalty, thus requiring families to live separately on their own land. The people very soon acquired various European traits concerning the land and learned to fence their holdings. Lakotas who still have land find that their individual tracts are too small for grazing purposes and usually too arid to farm. The allotment system created a problem not only of physical but of social isolation, and many a Lakota child learned to fear everyone except the few people seen daily on the lonely homestead.

Nevertheless, communities and villages, usually deriving from historic bands, persist (Feraca 1966). In part due to isolation, traditional religion in these communities continues to flourish. Even in the smaller, truly remote locales, often two or more church buildings can be found. The activities of the Christian congregations, like those of the participants in traditional religious meetings, are very strongly kinship oriented.

The reservations, open to external proselytizing from their very beginnings, were also influenced from within by native clergy and catechists.[6] Lately they have been visited by Seventh-Day Adventists, representatives of the Church of God, and other Protestant denominations. On both Pine Ridge and Rosebud roughly 60 percent of the population is Roman Catholic, with most of the rest divided among Protestant groups, and relatively few listed as members of the Native American (Peyote) Church.

The earlier clergy seem to have assumed one of two attitudes toward native practices and beliefs: either ignore them or stamp them out. Before the New Deal and John Collier's Indian Bureau policies, every assistance was rendered the missionaries in suppressing the Lakota religion. Dances and ceremonies of all types were attacked by the government, whether religious or not. However, the only ceremony officially banned was the Sun Dance. Medicine men and herbalists often practiced secretively and were sometimes arrested. The introduction of peyote in Lakota country greatly alarmed the clergy, despite the fact that the peyote dogma and ritual have a definite Christian character. On the whole, most of the clergy are quite unaware of the existence of many traditional religious groups and, moreover, would be surprised to learn that any of them are active or vital in the life of the Lakotas.[7]

All official objections to native religious practices were lifted during the Collier administration and under the atmosphere engendered by the Indian Reorganization Act of 18 June 1934 (*Statutes at Large* 1934, 48, 984).[8] The Native American Church was recognized, and some supposedly forgotten ceremonies were formally revived, including the Sun Dance.

TWO

THE SUN DANCE

Daniel Grass Rope arose from his seat amidst the spectators and gazed at the top of the Sun Dance pole. Lifting his cased pipe in one hand, this venerable patriarch with braided hair addressed *Wakhą́ Thą́ka* and the assembled Lakotas. He announced that he was approaching one hundred years of age, that a good thing was about to commence on this day, and that he desired that the many treaty promises be soon fulfilled (referring to the expected payment for the Black Hills). Old Grass Rope then smoked his pipe, calmly awaiting the entry of the dancers. He had traveled all the way from Lower Brule Reservation to the Pine Ridge Sun Dance, and he was not disappointed; the dance was very satisfactory, despite the fact that three of the four dancers were Northern Cheyennes in this ceremony held in 1954 (Feraca 1957).

Ben American Horse, also long haired and resplendent in a beaded and fringed shirt and leggings, then addressed his people. He did not hide the fact that he considered it something of a disgrace that only one tribal member could be found who was willing to undergo the sacrifice.[1] As with the previous speaker, a chorus of "*háu*" punctuated his remarks. A few minutes later, at about nine in the morning, an impressive and colorful procession emerged from the preparation tipi and walked into the dance lodge.

Frank Fools Crow led the group bearing a buffalo skull on a bed of sage. In absolute silence and with slow, deliberate steps the four dancers followed in single file, painted and with shawls wrapped around their waists and sage around their heads, wrists, arms, and ankles. A woman holding a small chokecherry shoot with cloth and tobacco offerings followed the dancers and was accompanied by a very aged individual in a disreputable black suit and hat, an assistant to the director. George Poor Thunder, a noted Pine Ridge medicine man (but Sičháǧu) and the director of this and some previous Sun Dances, was last in the single file. His graying braids and his old-time way of draping his blue blanket about him presented a picture of dignity. He bore the catlinite pipe to be used in the ceremony.

After they circled the pole clockwise, the skull was placed at the west side of the lodge. The pipe was leaned against one horn (usually a wooden rack is provided). The dancers, their backs to the pole, faced the skull as Poor Thunder directed the woman in placing the decorated chokecherry-shoot offering at the bottom of the pole. After a preliminary prayer-song by the director, during which most spectators covered their faces with one or both hands, the dancers turned to face the sun as their ordeal was about to commence. The mercury had already climbed past ninety, but these four dancers, one a Korean War veteran on crutches, were to have no food or water, and little rest, for the entire day. The singers began the first song to the accompaniment of a rolling drumbeat, recalling the thunderous herds that were once so plentiful; and when the beat changed, the Sun dancers began shrilling their eagle ulnar whistles and bobbing from their knees, while the lone, aged Lakota atypically lifted his feet one at a time. The rest of their bodies were virtually immobile.

No ceremonial of Lakota culture is as characteristic of that culture as the Sun Dance. The power concept, individualism, the warrior heritage, and the excesses so typically Lakota all have their place in this ceremony. The Sun Dance was adapted from the medicine-lodge ceremony of the Cheyennes. The activities and artifacts connected with the ceremony were borrowed whole and subjected to the individualism of the Lakotas. These groups, particularly the Oglálas, were instrumental in diffusing their version of the Sun Dance among other Plains tribes (Spier 1921, 494).[2] This new method of acquiring power, involving as it did bloodshed and colorful display, appealed greatly to the Lakota warriors. In some regard the Sun Dance is wholly unlike the various night ceremonies, which will be described in succeeding pages.

Wiwáyąg Wačípi (Sun Gazing Dance) is an appropriate term. Although other tribes like the Cheyennes refer, in English, to their medicine-lodge ceremonies as "Sun Dances," actually gazing at the sun is not an established feature. With the Lakotas gazing at the sun fulfills two requirements: invoking the power of the sun as a deity and inducing further torture, although of a bloodless nature. Torture as such was not a feature of the dance in this century prior to the 1960s, but, in explaining why the old dance was banned by the federal government, we will briefly outline the more common torments known in pre- and early-reservation days.

The torture, entirely voluntary, was so necessary to the old dance that, if there were no candidates to undergo the extreme forms, the piercing, the ceremony probably would not be held at all that year (Walker 1917, 61–62). True to that characteristic of the Lakotas which we can only call ostentation, many dancers elaborated on the length and nature of the suffering. A lesser form involved no more torture than that inflicted by making minute cuts in one of the dancers' limbs. In an extreme form, buffalo skulls were tied to thongs, the ends of which were fastened to the dancer's back muscles. A common practice was to attach the ends of two thongs to sticks skewering the chest muscles. The other ends of the thongs were tied by rope to the Sun Dance pole. The dancer would then strain against the thongs until his chest muscles were ripped. Still another form consisted in the dancer's being fastened with thongs to two or four stakes, the object being to free himself by tearing loose through his back or chest muscles or both. In 1960 a Sičháǧu dancer at Pine Ridge had the epidermis of one breast pierced in a token sacrifice and was attached to the pole. The following summer the same dancer, assisted by the same director, was very deeply pierced on the right breast, to the great edification of the Lakota spectators. A considerable effort attended the dancer's freeing himself of the skewer.[3]

Those whites who desired the quick transformation of the Lakotas were quite horrified at such proceedings and were, in addition, fearful about so many Lakotas gathered in one place. The Sun Dance, after years of pressure on the part of agency officials and missionaries, was officially banned in 1883 by a Bureau of Indian Affairs edict. A lukewarm event on Rosebud, the last of the nineteenth-century torture dances, was permitted in 1883 after the ban was issued. In 1881 the Oglálas and Sičhą́ǧus held a memorable dance at Pine Ridge in which more than forty dancers participated, the extraordinary number undoubtedly due to the Lakotas being advised that this was to have been the last dance.

Verbal accounts vary, and some are quite suspect, regarding torture dances held early in this century. I was told, for example, that at the very large Sun Dance at Rosebud in 1928, all of the many male participants were pierced. There was no piercing at this extensively photographed affair; the males simulated it by strap-like devices around their upper torsos attached by ropes to the pole. I remain extremely skeptical about dancers actually being pierced at any of the ceremonies reportedly conducted at remote locales on Pine Ridge in secret (the Sun Dance is a very public undertaking) in the early years of this century.

No two Sun Dances are exactly alike; often supposedly basic elements are subject to change. I have, for example, seen Sun Dances in which the candidates faced the four directions or the pole rather than follow the sun. The 1955 Pine Ridge Sun Dance, directed by Jesse White Lance, a Sičhą́ǧu medicine man, is the only ceremony I have ever witnessed in which all dancing positions faced the sun (Feraca 1957).[4]

There is some confusion regarding the date of the official revival of the Sun Dance on Pine Ridge Reservation. Most Oglálas will state that the first contemporary dance was held in 1934, when the entire celebration, including all other dances, was known as the First Annual Sun Dance. However, we have evidence that in the 1920s and earlier a few Sun Dances were held. A few old and middle-aged men and women constituted the typical Sun Dance group before the late 1950s. An atypical group was that of Lakota World War II veterans who danced in thanksgiving at the Northern Arapahoe medicine-lodge in 1946. From the first, although this is not true of such tribes as the Cheyennes and Arapahoes, very few Lakotas except the older men and women were interested in participating in the Sun Dance, even though the revived ceremony was devoid of bloodshed (with the possible exception of small flesh offerings). The prolonged preliminary rites involving fasting, certain taboos, and other avoidance measures on the part of the candidate are generally

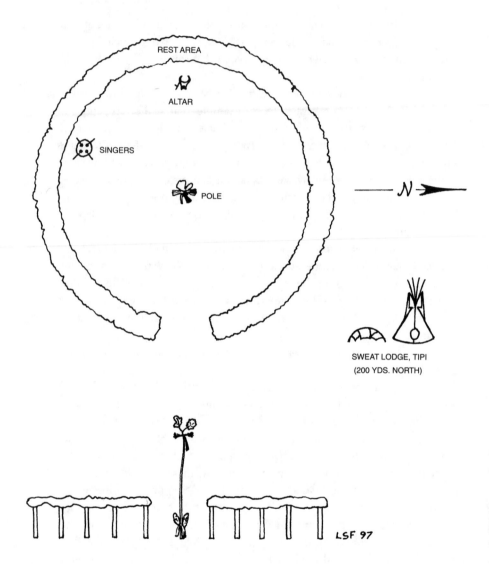

REST AREA

ALTAR

SINGERS

POLE

N

SWEAT LODGE, TIPI
(200 YDS. NORTH)

LSF 97

Sun Dance Lodge, Pine Ridge, 1954, top and side views (after Feraca 1963)

ignored, the only purificatory preliminary being the sweat bath. Even the injunction to abstain from food and drink during the dance is only loosely observed, and it is only recently that any younger men from Pine Ridge and Rosebud have offered themselves for the sacrifice.

Many Lakotas regard the annual Northern Arapahoe medicine-lodge ceremony held on the Wind River Reservation in Wyoming as the true Sun Dance. This attitude may be explained in light of Lakota values concerning the fast, which is often ignored in their own ceremony and is comparatively short in duration. The Arapahoes fast and dance for three or four days; the Lakotas have been known to consume full meals the night of the first day's dancing (that is, if the dance lasts for more than one day). As in the old times, no contemporary Lakota Sun Dances last more than two days, and, unlike in the Arapahoe version, no activities are continued through the night.[5] Most Lakotas who have witnessed the "Sun Dances" of other tribes are much impressed with the more formalized, more rigidly standardized rites common to many of these other ceremonies and largely unknown to the Lakotas.

By these very attitudes the Lakotas belie their disinterest in the Sun Dance. The truth of the matter is that what the old Lakota Sun Dance lacked in impressive formality it gained in various excesses, such as bloodshed. An Arapahoe Sun Dance leader reportedly declared that the Lakota version of the dance is older and more acceptable. The other tribes are able to maintain three- or four-day annual ceremonies completely devoted to a Sun Dance or medicine-lodge ceremony, but the Pine Ridge summer celebration features the Sun Dance for only the first day or two. The entire four-day (sometimes five-day) affair is advertised as the Sun Dance, but some Lakotas deliberately stay away until the Sun Dance itself is over. The great majority of the encamped people are much more interested in the Omaha or grass dancing, in which they participate in great numbers. When first visiting the Lakota reservations I was somewhat confused by the numerous persons who declared that they had "danced the Sun Dance." It soon became apparent that "dancing Omaha"—a strictly secular dance—at the Sun Dance celebration was meant.

A Sun Dance committee is formed to decide the dates of the celebration, select the Sun Dance director, and arrange for the printing and distribution of posters and the maintenance of the dance grounds situated just east of Pine Ridge village. This committee also attends to such mundane matters as the construction of public outhouses on the grounds and the grading of the road leading to the dance grounds from Highway 18.[6]

For some celebrations souvenir booklets are printed by order of the committee. These booklets are notorious for anachronisms and poor spelling. What interests us here are statements that maintain that the Sun Dance merely recalls the Lakota past and is in no way a religious ceremony. One year the dance was referred to by an announcer as a "reenactment." This is manifestly untrue, since no traditionalist, even in the capacity of a singer, will have anything to do with the ceremony itself unless he has some respect for the power of the dance. This fact remains, even though the candidates are often paid by the committee (later the tribal council). Omaha dancers are not paid, yet their numbers often exceed two hundred at a given time.

The actual labor on the part of the committee members (locally called "committees") begins about two weeks before the celebration. The dance lodge or "shade" is erected and the grounds thoroughly raked and cleared.[7] This lodge consists of two concentric circles of posts, the space between the inner and outer circles being covered with pine boughs to shelter spectators, with a portion at the west side for dancers' rest periods. Contrary to Brown's description obtained from Black Elk, the dance lodge is completely open to sunlight (Brown 1971, 80–81). The spokelike poles or rafters radiating from the center pole, so common to other Plains tribes, are not found in the Lakota dance lodge, but some Lakotas remembered such structures, as evidenced in the drawings in the Red Horse Owner Winter Count (Karol 1969, 39, 50).

Neither the candidates for the dance nor the director are usually concerned with the construction of the lodge. Not until the day before the Sun Dance itself do they enter the picture. Only then is the ceremonial tipi erected — either near the entrance of the lodge or at the rear — and the sweat lodge prepared. The tipi is well known today and needs no description; the sweat lodge and the rites of the sweat bath will be discussed below in conjunction with other ceremonies.

The Sun Dance pole (*čhąwákhą* or "holy tree") is selected on the afternoon of the day before the dance. As mentioned above, this pole does not function as a support for other poles. Among the Lakotas it is a cottonwood tree (*wáǧačhą*) stripped of all its branches except for those at the very top. The selection of and actual cutting and trimming of the pole are usually accomplished in a manner quite perfunctory as compared with pre- and early-reservation customs. Only a minimum of spectators attend the activities connected with the preparation of the pole. The only vestige that remains of a ceremonial nature in the cutting of the pole is that children or old men of good character are occasionally asked to deliver the final blows that fell the tree and to trim it of any lower branches. I have heard coarse jokes made by the men in reference to the former practice of having a virgin cut the pole.[8]

Contemporary Lakotas may not know many of the rites connected with the earlier Sun Dance, but few individuals seem unaware of the proscription concerned with transporting the pole. It is never supposed to touch the ground (which is virtually impossible) until actually set upright within the dance lodge. The pole used in the separate dance (an extraordinary phenomenon in itself) held at the Oglala community before the tribal celebration (Pine Ridge Sun Dance) in the summer of 1954 was unceremoniously tied to a truck and dragged to the dance site. This flagrant act on the part of those who transported the pole was duly noted by the outraged elders. It is significant that the incident immediately became a topic for conversation throughout the reservation.

As a result of exhaustive research into the matter of decorating the pole, the conclusion is inescapable that there has always been diversity in both early and modern times. A brush bundle, a human and a buffalo figure, and a red cloth banner stand out as items most commonly used, but even these are not considered indispensable.[9] In 1954 all of the abovementioned items were tied near the top of the pole. The following year the pole was decorated with various colored cloths. An enlarged and awkward-looking brush bundle was featured, but the rawhide figures, both human and buffalo, were omitted. Different leaders directed these ceremonies.

All cloth offerings, called *wa'úyąpi* by the Lakotas, are survivals of the trading era, when cloth of any kind was highly esteemed. A bit of tobacco is

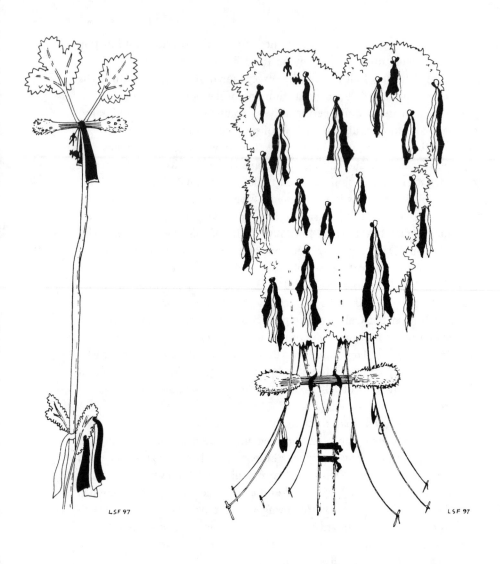

LSF 97

LSF 97

(Left) Sun Dance "Pole," Pine Ridge, 1954 (after Feraca 1957); (right) Bear Shield "Tree," Wounded Knee, 1996; staked ropes are for piercing

tied in at least one corner of each such cloth. The consensus among Lakotas is that for the Sun Dance a red banner is appropriate for the top of the pole (before trade cloth was available a finely tanned buffalo calfskin was used), and any variety of colored cloths may be tied or placed near the bottom after the pole is erected.[10] The rawhide figures, if used, represent to the modern Lakotas a bull buffalo and an enemy soldier. In early reservation days, and even before, these figures were often shot down before the dance actually commenced. Their origin lies with the Cheyennes; the Lakotas are not usually concerned about such historical matters (Feraca 1957, 47–49).

The brush bundle, composed of chokecherry shoots (*čhąpáhu*), is tied either horizontally near the top of the pole in a fork or to the trunk itself. It is quite clear that among the Cheyennes, who make use of several brush bundles, they represent the Thunderbird's nest (G. Dorsey 1905, 117). For the Lakotas the Thunderbird or Winged Deity is *Wakįyą*, an extremely powerful being who creates thunder, lightning, strong winds, rainstorms, and hail. Probably very few of the Lakotas of old actually thought of the brush bundle borrowed from the Cheyennes as a nest. Walker's "fetish of the Sun Dance" conveys nothing in this respect (1917, 109).[11]

Very few Lakotas regard the chokecherry bundle as anything other than a Christian symbol. *Wakįyą*'s nest became the crossbar of a cross, and many Sun Dance poles certainly do resemble a cross. At a dance at Rosebud in 1958 the chokecherry shoots were not even bound into a nestlike bundle. Only two young shoots were tied horizontally to the pole. This may, however, have been due to haste, since the pole was transported and erected during heavy rain.

Many Lakotas consider the Sun Dance as thoroughly Christian in origin. They cite the similarity between the crucifix and the Sun Dance pole, and they equate the suffering of the dancers with Christ's suffering and the concept of penance. Considered historically this is of course without basis. Considered ethnologically it is of prime importance to anyone attempting to understand the dynamics of contemporary Lakota culture.

To vow participation in the Sun Dance is not an easy decision for the Lakotas. The candidates are rarely considered courageous or of exceptional character, and very little prestige is accorded the individual or his family. In 1955 a dancer at Pine Ridge was arrested on a charge of fraud as soon as the one-day ceremony was completed. He was led away by tribal police while still in costume.[12]

South Dakota is hot in the summer, often unbearably so. The Sun Dance song that asks the candidates if they want water, and then tells them that none is to be had, is reminiscent of the old days yet appropriate today. It is agonizing to dance in a fixed position. For the male dancers, constant blowing on the eagle-bone whistles, particularly while facing the sun, is in itself a torture.[13] At the Rosebud Sun Dance of 1958 an aged woman dancer suddenly slumped to the ground. She was barely conscious but was not removed to the shelter of the tipi until the entire rite of asking the singers for a rest (described later) was completed.

Added to the lack of advantages for the candidates and the discomforts of actually participating in the ceremony is the censure of many people in the area, both Catholic and Protestant. To many Lakotas, the term "Christian" refers to the rather puritanical individual who allows no intoxicants in his home, is a regular churchgoer, and who does not "Indian dance" or "white dance" on any occasion. These individuals can be expected to criticize anyone who might participate in the Sun Dance.

Motives for dancing are many and varied. It is expected that every candidate will pray for the general well-being of the people. It is also expected that during the ceremony, or soon afterward, a dancer will receive a vision. The forms that these visions take will be discussed later. Every dancer, however, does have a distinctly personal reason for offering the sacrifice. Possibly the most unusual motive for gazing at the sun in all Lakota history was that of William Spotted Crow, when in 1952 he threatened to pray for a Democratic victory in Republican South Dakota. At the last moment Spotted Crow relented and, as the newspapers reported it, "lifted the curse." The young Cheyenne cripple who danced in 1954 was undoubtedly concerned about his health, but he also prayed for the safe return of other soldiers from overseas. His companions from his own tribe had in mind, among other things, their own safe return from Korea. In recent years various individuals, both men and women,

Portion of Sun Dance Group, Pine Ridge, 1961, with bottom of pole at right

have danced because either they or close relatives were ill or had recovered from a serious ailment sometime during the year. In the old torture dance it is known that a few young blades underwent the torments to impress some young female; no such motive is possible today.[14]

There is good reason to believe that in pre- and early-reservation days the announcement of one's intention to dance was the occasion of much proud gift-giving on the part of one's immediate family. More give-aways would be seen during the ceremony, both the number and quality of gifts seemingly dependent upon the character of the suffering the candidate would undergo. This practice has largely been abandoned. In fact, the identities of the dancers are rarely known until they enter the sweat lodge. Nor is it expected that the individual will reveal a motive for dancing. Merely because I aided one of the principal dancers, an elderly gentleman, in 1956 in decorating the Sun Dance pole, I was asked if I would like to dance.[15] The invitation was graciously declined. What is significant is that this gesture was made only half an hour before the ceremony began.

"Haphazard," say many white observers of the Lakota Sun Dance. I say rather that their seemingly haphazard actions are merely manifestations of the lack of rigid standardization in Lakota ceremonialism. For example, a buffalo skull often used in the Pine Ridge Sun Dance could be found at any time, except during the dance, in front of an automobile parts store in nearby White Clay, Nebraska. Whistles of the wooden toy variety have been used by dancers, and cardboard sun emblems have been worn, suspended from a thong around the neck.

A description of the somewhat complicated rite of obtaining a rest during the dance will serve to illustrate some of the individualistic traits exhibited in the course of the ceremony. A brief respite is obtained when the pipe resting on or near the buffalo skull is ceremoniously offered to the singers. While the singers smoke the pipe, the dancers retire to a reserved area under the shade, just behind the buffalo skull altar. I have observed diverse ceremonial methods of handling this pipe (Feraca 1957, 103–6). In one Pine Ridge ceremony the director placed the pipe in the dancer's hands and then conducted him at a walk to the singers. The pipe was offered to the singers after three feints, a singer touching it at the fourth feint. The pipe was then rocked back and forth four times (the usual prescribed ritual number) until the dancer relinquished his hold upon it. The following year the director would periodically approach one of the dancers, all of whom carried pipes, and the dancer would hop toward the singers and make three feints before relinquishing the pipe. At this dance one pipe, and occasionally more than one, was always resting on a rack behind the skull. The frequency and length of these rest periods depend entirely upon the director's wishes.

In recent years, many accusations have been heaped upon the heads of those participants in the dance, including singers, who have been seen eating and drinking during the ceremony. While fasting may not be required of the singers, it is expected of them. In 1954 I observed the singers eating watermelon

Offering the Pipe to the Singers, Pine Ridge, 1955

during rest periods, at the same time complaining about the *wašíčhу* visitor with a raucous voice who had provided the watermelon.

Despite the varying degrees of hostility to the Sun Dance displayed by many of the Lakotas who camp by the thousands on the grounds, there are crowds of spectators. They are interested, if only to observe "how bad they're doing it." Even Christians would at least mildly approve of the young Cheyenne who danced on one leg while he supported himself with crutches. The dancer who does not remove the whistle from his lips will inspire vocal approval from the assembled Lakotas, as will the dancer who gazes almost constantly at the sun. In 1958 the Sičháǧus held their Second Annual Sun Dance amidst great hostility from many communities on Rosebud Reservation. Even the date, 3 July, was unacceptable to most of the people. The six dancers, including the director himself, put on a good show, but most of those encamped at the site ignored the proceedings (they were awaiting the Omaha dancing that would follow). On the same day a much more popular event, an Omaha Dance, was being held in another part of the reservation.

"This is just for tourists" is a remark often heard from Lakota spectators at the Sun Dance. In a sense this attitude is quite unjustified. I witnessed Pine Ridge Sun Dances that attracted relatively few non-Indian spectators, yet the complaint that the ceremony is a tourist affair is commonly encountered.[16]

A narrated documentary film, later shown to television audiences by Walt Disney, was made during the 1956 Sun Dance at Pine Ridge. Those Lakotas who believe that it is impossible to develop films of Cheyenne and Arapahoe ceremonies were, predictably, strengthened in their attitude that the Lakota Sun Dance is not authentic. The following year the Rosebud Sun Dance committee pointedly stated in its advertising posters that the dance to be held on that reservation was not for the sake of moviemakers.

THREE

THE VISION QUEST

Hąbléčheya, "crying for a dream," is the Lakota term for the widely practiced North American vision quest. *Hąbléčheya* may be defined as the deliberate seeking of a vision after previously purifying oneself with the sweat bath and undergoing, in solitude, the torments of complete abstinence until the desired effect is achieved. Such an effect may be the appearance of buffalo, coyotes, elk, or practically any mammal, bird, insect, or reptile known to the Lakotas. Lakotas also consider beings in human or somewhat human form and the ghosts of humans and animals as fit subjects for bona fide visions. The creature or personage appearing to the fasting Lakota during the vision quest usually appears in subsequent vision quests and functions as a continuing source of power.

In speaking of *hąbléčheya* in this chapter, we are primarily discussing the making of a medicine man. Before proceeding, some definitions are in order. The term "dream" (*hąblé,* in Lakota the same as "vision") will be used only in reference to an unsought or unexpected visitation. The nature of visions, as distinct from dreams, is that they are usually sought after, the dream that is cried for, whether occurring while the subject is conscious or not. Many Lakotas have fainted as a result of prolonged fasting and have, while in that state, obtained the desired vision. As will be explained in some detail below, many dreams of a religious nature are quite frightening and in no way desirable to the subject, although a vision may be feverishly sought.[1] The apparition in the vision is welcome only if regarded as an end to the distress caused by the initial dream. The Lakotas usually distinguish between the unsought dream and that resulting from the practice of *hąbléčheya.*

A medicine man emerges from the rank and file in the following manner, after a fairly standardized pattern of action (basically unchanged from the prereservation era) has been fulfilled. His introduction to the supernatural usually begins in early childhood when his older female relatives, particularly his grandmother, frighten him with the Lakota versions of the bogeyman, often called *číči* man (sometimes the *wašíčhu* is included among those who "will get you if you're bad"). By the time a boy has reached his early teens he has attended religious meetings or at least heard innumerable stories of power. He will undoubtedly have a close relative who claims to have been cured of some illness by a medicine man. However, it is practically unheard of that a Lakota boy will aspire to be one of the practitioners he has heard so much about.[2]

The dream that sets him on the path, if involving any of the creatures or objects known to Lakota cosmology, will be recognized by the subject as spiritual in nature. He will then consult a medicine man or aged person knowledgeable in such matters who will interpret his dream for him and prescribe the vision quest. After a sweat bath is held, in which the subject and his mentor participate, the candidate then ascends a lonely hill with articles such as a filled pipe and some cloth and tobacco offerings to place on sticks at the site of his fasting. The candidate usually strips to a breechcloth or shorts while seeking his vision. During the day and most of the night he will pray and wail for pity from the spirits. For most Lakotas the loneliness in itself must be terrible. Passersby, if any, will completely ignore him. The mentor may visit him daily.[3]

The candidate sleeps on a bed of sage that his mentor prepares for him, but food and water are taboo. However, during the more lengthy vision quests, candidates have been known to consume water in small quantities, at least in the form of herbal tea. A few minutes' "stand" constitutes the shortest quest, four days and nights the longest. A stand of very short duration does not require any ceremonial preparation and is usually practiced by women.[4] Often the length is not specified, and the sufferer will pass days in attempting to gain the desired vision. On the other hand, some have given up after an unrewarding night.

At the end of the specified period, or as soon as the vision has been granted, the candidate reports to his mentor. During the closing sweat bath the subject will disclose his vision, if he has one to disclose. If favorable, he is free to immediately begin practicing the arts of the medicine man. What he must often do is ally himself with an experienced medicine man until he is proficient at conducting whatever ceremony or ceremonies are associated with his vision. Occasionally, fathers pass such knowledge on to sons who have obtained satisfactory visions.

The rather brief outline above makes no provision for those who have denied the "call." A noted practitioner from Kyle on the Pine Ridge Reservation, Jesse Stead, ignored his initial dream about thunder until it was repeated four times. At that point he was so impressed by the dream itself, and by fear of being struck by lightning (punished by *Wakíyą*), that he consulted "the old people and medicine men." This practitioner and most other consultants state that those who have sought visions unsuccessfully were either morally unfit or did not complete the fast. If the seeker has no vision to report he will either try again or be advised that he is evidently not to be selected as a recipient for power.

Hąblécheya is practiced not only by medicine men but by any person, including women, who wishes to be advised by the spiritual powers. A woman was requested by her ailing husband and a medicine man known as Blue Legs to make the vision quest, in this instance partly to offer a sacrifice on her husband's behalf. Accordingly, she began the vigil on a hill a short distance from her house, but she returned that night, not having completed the rite for fear of ghosts.

If the afflicted (in many instances the term is appropriate) person does not prepare for *hąblécheya*, the unsought dream will recur and possibly assume the proportions of a nightmare. Lightning, it is believed, will endanger him and his immediate family, and various other misfortunes, such as the death of horses or cattle, may be in store. A middle-aged Oglála dreamed of a black horse and dog, which are associated with thunder. The dream was ignored and he forgot the matter. When it recurred he was convinced that he was called upon to "clown dance," a phenomenon to be discussed later. Apparently his older relatives advised him to await further developments, and, since the dream ceased to torment him—and since he was not attracted to the native religious beliefs in the first place—he gave up the whole thing as a mistake. The man from Kyle who had expressed his concern upon receiving his initial dream was a practicing Catholic and aspiring to attend college when called to the ranks of those specialists known as "*yuwípi* men." In his own words, until he decided to perform the rite of *hablécheya*, he was "crawling around in darkness," meaning spiritual ignorance (a Christian metaphor).

The Lakotas believe that many medicine men have had visions and dreams that were improperly interpreted or were not conducive to the gaining of power at all. Other Lakotas, among them medicine men, state that those who dabble in ceremonies not associated with their visions are responsible for such happenings as Sun Dances that were inconclusive due to rain and hail. Moisture is always welcome in South Dakota but never in the immediate vicinity of a religious ceremony. A prominent healer among the Oglálas blamed one of his colleagues for several unsatisfactory Sun Dances. During a Pine Ridge Sun Dance celebration, after the dance itself was completed, the director's son-in-law died in the encampment. The consensus is that this man's powers, as revealed in his vision, did not include the ability to conduct the Sun Dance. Others say he simply made too many mistakes, such as not placing the proper "tokens" and offerings on the pole.

Although there are many variations on this theme, in the dream the candidate might see himself performing the actions of a medicine man, perhaps conducting a specific ceremony. As said, the vision usually takes the form of an elaboration upon the original dream, in which a supernatural being instructs the candidate. The instruction may include the prayers and rites of a particular ceremony and the use of herbs. Many Lakotas, themselves devotees of a particular ceremony, maintain that the candidate learns the use of herbs from experienced medicine men and women and invents his own prayer-songs. It may be worthwhile to mention here that while questioning a very cooperative consultant, I was seriously asked if I was interested in becoming a medicine man. I was advised of the vicissitudes of such a life but was not asked if I had experienced a religious dream.

All of the medicine men fast at least once a year, usually during warm weather, until a satisfactory vision is achieved. Mark Big Road, a well-respected healer, fasts more than once during a season. One may understandably wonder at such a severe exercise, but the Lakotas believe that medicine men learn from each new vision; that is, they acquire more power (although one practitioner advised me that he had lost the right to use a particular design he had often drawn in his earthen altar). Those who conduct specific ceremonies often mention some aspects of their original vision, or the latest obtained, at the beginning of each meeting.

An absorbing trait in the Lakota religious pattern is the conception that the medicine man possesses various spirits revealed in the visions. It follows, therefore, that the more spirits owned by the medicine man, the more powerful his ceremonial actions will be. A corollary to this is found in the belief that the more spirits or objects possessed and used by him, the more dangerous he is to himself, his family, and society at large. Thus, despite the employment of the words "has" or "uses," in English or Lakota, the medicine man never entirely controls these forces. Religion to the Lakotas is a dangerous business. What is benevolent can become malevolent due to many causes, even if the medicine man himself is of good will.

Black magic or magic performed for the sake of evil is rare. The Lakotas fear the power itself as much as its deliberate misuse.[5] Some individuals, after being rewarded with a satisfactory vision, have enjoyed but brief periods as medicine men. What most Americans would call ordinary bad luck, on their part or that of their families, has convinced some men to cease all activity connected with the ceremonies. An Oglála declared that he no longer assisted medicine men by singing with a drum at meetings because "they never know what they're going to get." He was referring to malevolent power. Sometimes jestingly, more often seriously, I have been warned by many Lakotas not to "fool with those things. You'll be lightning-struck."

The vision often specifies, in addition to purely ceremonial phenomena, certain other elements, such as taboos. A well-known medicine man among the Oglálas was warned not to fall in love. Others have been exhorted never to keep money or gifts rendered them for their services. One injunction specifies that the medicine man may not live with his immediate family, due to the volatile nature of the power he has received.

A *mathó waphíye* (bear doctor) who lived on the Pine Ridge Reservation was instructed by a bear spirit in the use of herbs. This ceremony, very old among the Lakotas, evidently was limited to curing. The man I interviewed, a grandson of the bear doctor who as a boy acted as his assistant, stated that the vision specified that after curing a certain large number of persons his grandfather would die. The prophecy is reported to have been fulfilled.

One practitioner of a ceremony devoted to *hųkála*, an elder or an ancestor, obtained his power after ghosts (*wanáǧi*), some in animal form, appeared to him. This healer, David Day, was of the somewhat rare type who dealt with malevolent spirits although they themselves may have been of good character. The concept of association with *wakhą́šiča* (bad holy things) may be compared to a Christian's praying to Satan for a good purpose, such as the welfare of a sick relative. Blue Legs, a much respected medicine man who was evidently not associated with any particular ceremony, but who was regarded as powerful even after becoming blind, was lost for a lengthy period, during which time a coyote appeared to inform him that he would receive power. Since he was alone, and in a half-starved condition, the basic requirements of the vision quest were unwittingly fulfilled. I was not informed, however, about any initial dream that Blue Legs may have experienced.

The vision may include, among other items previously mentioned, instruction about what is required of a good medicine man. Ideally, these requirements add considerably to the many injunctions by which a practitioner is to abide. He is not to demand any specified payment, whether in cash or kind, for his services. In actuality, for difficult cases such as severe illness or the finding of a valuable object that has been lost, he may receive horses or cash. He is to pray constantly for the general good and welfare of the people and in all things function as a good example to his tribe. He is not to drink and not to be seen in the company of drunks. He is to constantly remind himself, or others will do so, that lightning will strike the greedy or uncharitable practitioner just as quickly as it will consume one who tampers with those sacred things not of his domain.

The Church of the Body of Jesus Christ, a local Evangelical sect of strictly Lakota origin (founded by a Cheyenne River man) that appeared in the late 1950s at Wolf Creek on Pine Ridge, prescribes a particular vision quest. The members are exhorted to fast for one night with a Bible before them. A successful quest will result in the underlining of a passage in the Bible during the course of the night.

Hạbléčheya constitutes one of the core elements of Lakota religion; it could exist, and does exist, irrespective of any other ceremony. Its importance to the Lakotas may be summed up in the words of an aged Oglála, Mrs. Mary Fast Horse, who emphatically declared, "I believe in God . . . and holy things like *hạbléčheya.*"[6]

FOUR

YUWÍPI

The most popular traditional religious ceremony on the Pine Ridge and Rosebud Reservations is *yuwípi*, named after the practice of tying and wrapping the medicine man.[1] Although *yuwípi* translates in English as "they wrap him," the spirits used or owned by these specialists are referred to as *yuwípi*, the etymology being ignored by the Lakotas.

Membership in *yuwípi*, a term to be used cautiously although Lakotas are often quite liberal in this respect, is determined solely by attendance at "meetings" or "ceremonies." Any Lakota who attends at least one meeting during the year can be classified as a *yuwípi* devotee. Initiations are unknown, except in the case of one *yuwípi wičháša* (*yuwípi* man) confiding in another or instructing a neophyte. The devotees are participants insofar as the adult males usually join in the sweat bath preceding the ceremony, and all "help the *yuwípi* man sing" while the meeting is in progress.

Yuwípi falls into the category of the Plains Indian darkened-room or darkened-tent night ceremonies involving spirits, usually diminutive. This type of ceremony, with the tying and subsequent freeing of the medicine man, long existed on the plains and prairies and in the woodlands and is known to many far-flung tribes. It is my belief that the original *yuwípi* men specialized in being untied by small, hairy, manlike spirits. The practice of *yuwípi* seems closely related to the Ojibwe and Cree Shaking-Tent Rite and may be derived from it. This Woodland practice involves tying and wrapping the medicine man and placing him in a small, bark-covered "tent." During the course of the ceremony the bark structure will violently shake or sway. Some *yuwípi* men seek visions while securely bound and wrapped, and in instances known to me the *yuwípi* men, while so wrapped, fasted in covered sweat lodges.

A South Dakota State College bulletin describes *yuwípi* as marginal to Lakota religion and in that sense to be equated with the Native American Church (Malan and Jesser 1959, 48–49). With this I must disagree. *Yuwípi* is very widespread and embodies all the basic elements of Lakota religion, whereas peyotism lacks many of these. Peyotism is not fundamentally derived from the power concept and not associated with the plethora of traditional sources of power. Lakotas who are not in any manner personally involved in traditional religious practices are nevertheless usually loathe to condemn ceremonies like *yuwípi*. Many of these same individuals vehemently reject the use of peyote and do not exhibit traditional fear and respect toward the Native American Church and its leadership. Others, with no hesitancy, fully participate in both medicine men's ceremonies and peyotism. This discussion will be resumed when peyotism is covered in another chapter.

Since I wish to use *yuwípi* as a basis for discussing other ceremonies and medicine men, I will describe in detail a meeting witnessed by myself and Walter Karp, my fellow student from Columbia University. Someone who wishes the aid of any medicine man approaches him with a pipe or some Bull Durham tobacco. The practitioner will listen to the story and decide whether to take the case or not (they may smoke only after making a favorable decision). If the medicine man specializes in *yuwípi* he will instruct the seeker to prepare a feast for a meeting and to prepare the cloth and tobacco offerings. In 1956 Walter Karp and I enlisted the aid of an old man who introduced us to a *yuwípi* man who was planning to hold a meeting at the old man's house. It became necessary for us to give a member of the house-owner's family money to purchase goods for the "feed." By this act we reluctantly became the "promoters" of the ceremony. Fortunately, the conduct of the meeting was in no way adversely affected by our participation.

The entire ceremony, including the sweat-bath rite, described here is referred to as the Loafer Camp meeting since it was held at the Loafer Camp or Red Cloud community on the Pine Ridge Reservation in June 1956. Readers of this account must bear in mind that this is the method by which a particular medicine man conducted the meeting at a particular time. He, like many others, has been known to change some features of his own ceremony.

THE *INÍKAǦAPI*, OR SWEAT BATH

Iníkaǧapi ("they revitalize themselves") is undoubtedly one of the oldest rituals known to the Lakotas and was practiced long before reaching the high plains. It precedes practically every religious ceremony held in good weather and is even more often held for its own sake. It is rarely conducted as a purely salutary activity. *Iníkaǧapi*, or in its shorter form *inípi*, is primarily a religious rite for prayer and purification rather than a healthful exercise.

The sweat lodge (*iníthi*) is often found near the houses of older Lakotas. The one in our host's yard was constructed, as is typical, of willows bent to form an igloolike framework about six feet in diameter and four feet in height. Colored cloth offerings and Durham sacks from previous baths were tied to the framework. The entrance to the lodge was at the west; an earthen mound, representing the earth itself, was about three feet from the entrance, and the fire pit was situated about seven feet from this mound, all in a straight line. The entrance of the sweat lodge may face either east or west. The owner or builder may favor a particular direction or orientation (usually to the east), which is typical of Lakota individualism.

The fire was started by the aged house owner at about six in the evening. The limestones placed at the bottom of the pit were selected only for their heat-resistant properties. Unlike the practice of many traditionalists, there was absolutely no ceremony connected with the gathering of the firewood or the starting of the fire. Paper, broken boxes, and wood were piled on top of the stones. Kerosene was poured on and ignited with a match.

Our companion and interpreter, Victor Grass, offered himself as fire tender or doorkeeper. This pleased our host, but our reluctance to partake of the bath itself did not. It was pointed out to us that as promoters of the ceremony we should enter the lodge when all was ready. Several men now arrived and began to undress. A single canvas had been placed over the frame before the fire was started. Quilts were placed over this by the other men.

Constant joking was indulged in by all present; included among the remarks were many humorous references to the salutary nature of the bath. George Plenty Wolf, the *yuwípi* man, arrived less than an hour after the fire was started. He brought cloth and tobacco offerings and, after tying these to the framework, began to scatter about the floor of the lodge sage that the children had gathered nearby. He then returned to the house to get a small pipe with an L-shaped or elbow catlinite bowl. This pipe and its case were handled with sage and laid against the earthen mound, the stem pointing toward the fire.

The *yuwípi* man called for a metal bucket of water and a dipper. Five of the Lakotas present, all men, entered the lodge on their hands and knees, most of them with their shorts on, which they removed upon entering. The house owner waved his arms to the sun before entering in an effort to prevent the rain that was threatening.

After seating himself to the right of the entrance and placing the bucket before him, the *yuwípi* man requested six stones. Before removing his clothes one of the men had stated that solemnity and silence were to accompany the placing of these first six stones into the hole at the center of the lodge, the number six relating to the four cardinal directions, the zenith, and the nadir. Some of the participants continued to joke and talk, however.

The fire tender carried the stones with a pitchfork and then secured the quilts over the entrance. After some water was poured on the stones, the *yuwípi* man intoned the first of several rhymed prayers in an archaic type of speech. As the steam filled the lodge and the participants slapped and rubbed themselves with sage, the *yuwípi* man addressed *thųkášila* (paternal grandfather), which is the vocative for most of the beings known to Lakota cosmology. *Thųkášila Wakhą́ Thą́ka* is a common form, but this kinship term is never employed in Christian prayer. The *yuwípi* are always addressed in this manner. Each topic was preceded by the salutation "*Hói thųkášila*," and the full statement or verse was answered "*háu*" by all of the other participants.

The *yuwípi* man prayed for the fire tender, the promoters and their families, wild animals and birds, children, and servicemen, specifying those stateside, overseas, and traveling across the water. He included *Wakhą́ Thą́ka* in his verses. Another stone was called for, and at this time I decided to enter the lodge with a jovial latecomer who arrived equipped with his washcloth and towel. Definite approval accompanied our entrance, the *yuwípi* man stating that all was now quite well. The heat inside the lodge was almost unbearable, but this in no way affected the excellent voice of the principal singer, who sat at the rear of the lodge. The singing was started on a very high pitch with the others loudly joining in. The *yuwípi* man provided accompaniment by rapidly striking the bucket with the dipper. Most of the songs had few words; others consisted entirely of vocables.

The *yuwípi* man intoned another rhymed prayer. More singing was followed by more hot stones and more steam, after which, to the great relief of the ethnology student, the flap was opened and the *yuwípi* man ceremonially passed water. From the dipper, each took a sip or two, beginning with the individual to the left of the doorway. To accomplish this the dipper was first passed counterclockwise around the circle. Each spoke and was responded to in the same way as in smoking minutes later. The *yuwípi* man then requested the pipe. Since the wind was quite strong the previously filled pipe was lit not by the fire tender but by the man sitting across from the *yuwípi* man, to the left of the entrance. The pipe was held in both hands, bowl away from the body and stem pointed upward. The pipe was passed clockwise in the traditional manner, and after each participant smoked he said "*mithákuye oyás'į*" ("my relatives all"). The others responded "*háu*" while rubbing sage on their glistening bodies. After the *yuwípi* man finished smoking he reached out and replaced the pipe on the mound. The doorway was secured by the fire tender and the sweating resumed.

Rhymed prayers and more group singing followed until the hottest and largest stone was requested by the medicine man. The expressions of approval were very enthusiastic as all the remaining water was poured on. The pipe was again passed and thus ended the *iníkağapi*. Unlike the old-time practice it is now rare for the participants to drench themselves with cold water upon leaving the lodge. The house owner again waved his arms to the setting sun as we dressed. The *yuwípi* meeting was to begin shortly.

THE LOAFER CAMP *YUWÍPI* MEETING

Women in the house prepared food for the feast during and after the sweat bath. All cooking, done at one end of the large, single-room house, was completed by the time the meeting began, which was at ten o'clock. The entire affair, including the feast, lasted until just before midnight on a Saturday. Nine adult males were present, but no teenage boys; several teenage girls accompanied their mothers. Women and small children numbered more than twenty.

Preparation of the Room

Most of the furniture had been moved outside the house, bedrolls being placed against two of the walls as seats. A large quilt, later to be used in wrapping the *yuwípi* man, was hanging on a nail in the central pillar of the room. When we entered the room the house-owner's daughter, who was also the wife of the principal singer and assistant, was busily tacking tarpaper and canvas over the windows. The door was open, but tarpaper and blankets were ready to be placed over it. Light was provided by a single kerosene lantern. All Catholic religious pictures had been removed from the walls; however, a small rosary was overlooked (or possibly deliberately left in place).

Prior to shutting and covering the door, the devotees seated themselves on the bedrolls, the men, including those with drums, sitting on one side of the room and the women and children on the other. The men removed their hats, a Christian gesture of respect observed long before the 1950s and seen also during outdoor ceremonies when strictly religious songs are sung that actually contain prayers.

Preparation of the Altar and Sacred Area

While the room was prepared and the devotees were seating themselves, the *yuwípi* man took his ceremonial articles from an old suitcase and began arranging them on the wooden floor. On a piece of paper little more than a foot square, he poured earth and then smoothed it into a circle with a spotted eagle feather. One large tin can and six smaller ones, all bearing their labels, had been filled with earth and arranged behind the earthen altar (*makhákaǧapi*) along the south wall. Into these smaller cans were placed sticks about three feet long to which were tied cloth offerings containing a bit of tobacco. The larger can held a longer staff with the Lakota symbol representing all that is *wakhą́*, a red porcupine-quilled circle with a cross within it. A tiny skin-pouch of medicine was attached to the center. Dangling below the symbol were two spotted tail feathers of the mature golden eagle. Surrounding this staff were four short sticks bearing black, red, yellow, and white strips of cloth containing tobacco, which symbolized the four-in-one relationship found in *Wakhą́ Thą́ka*.[2] The number four refers, in its simplest interpretation, to the four directions. All four directions together insure the presence of *Wakhą́ Thą́ka*. The zenith and nadir need not be represented.

Why the *yuwípi* man took the trouble to arrange these offerings along the wall is uncertain, since he later removed all the sticks, with the attached offerings, and held them over the steam bucket brought in from the fire by a singer. The articles were thus purified as water was poured onto the hot stones in the bucket. The large can, with its original offerings and symbol, remained immediately behind the earthen altar; the other cans were placed about the room, outlining a rectangle. The *yuwípi* man maintained a definite pattern in placing the cans with their colored cloths or "flags." Four of the cloths (black, red, yellow, and white) represented the cardinal points (west, north, east, and south, respectively). The other two cloths, blue and green, represented the zenith (sky) and nadir (earth).

Čhąlí wapháȟta ("tied-tobacco" pouches, also called "rosaries") were arranged on the floor behind the cans. These commonly used ceremonial items are made of minute squares of cloth containing no more than a few grains of tobacco. The miniature bags are all tied with the same piece of cotton string. The length of *čhąlí wapháȟta* laid on the floor measured a few yards, each of the 405 pinches of tobacco constituting separate prayers and offerings to an equal number of spirits (in a practical sense such a length is needed to enclose the sacred area fully).

Within the sacred area the *yuwípi* man arranged a cellophane package of herbs, which were not used; two small gourdlike, rawhide rattles (*wagmúha*); and a length of braided sweet grass (*wačhą́ǧa*). An eagle-bone whistle, also

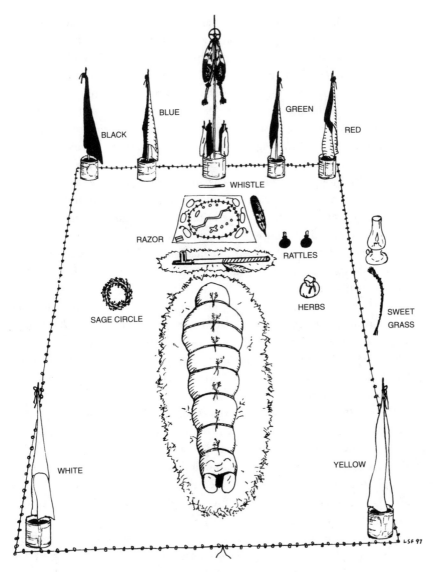

Yuwípi Sacred Area, Loafer Camp Meeting, 1956 (after Feraca 1963)

unused, was placed between the large can and the earthen altar, and a catlinite pipe with a T-shaped or prowed bowl and a stem decorated with porcupine quills was solemnly placed in front of the altar on a bed of sage.

At this point everyone, including small children, who had not participated in the sweat bath filed clockwise by the steam bucket and returned to their seats. As this purificatory rite was held, the *yuwípi* man rolled up the sleeves of his shirt and repeated some aspects of his vision. He announced that he would make use of lightning medicine, speaking entirely in Lakota (as did everyone else during the meeting, except myself and one of the singers who occasionally interpreted for me). The medicine man, as he concluded his initial speech, drew the appropriate lightning and other designs in the earthen altar with his index finger. As three of the women returned from the steam bucket they placed offerings of Bull Durham sacks, *chąlí waphá ̇hta*, and a razor blade on the altar. The medicine man outlined the earth circle with the tobacco strings and placed the Durham sacks around the altar after stripping the papers from them.

Sage was passed to the left by the principal singer, and each person in the room, including the *yuwípi* man, placed a bit over the right ear. Warning me to keep the sage, my friend Oliver Red Cloud explained that by doing so, "the *yuwípi* will know you." All participants were handed an aromatic dried flower, of a species unknown to me, with which they were to rub themselves as an added protection.

The sacred area and all of the devotees were further protected and purified by the singer-assistant, who lit one end of the sweet-grass rope with the lantern flame and waved it around the room. Everything was purified, including the altar, the prayer cloths, or *wa'ų́yąpi*, and the heads of everyone present. During this purification the *yuwípi* man twisted a circle of sage from the pile thrown into the sacred area by one of the men and placed this symbol on the floor. This circle or hoop represents the people. The medicine man filled the pipe without lifting it from the floor. With a quick flourish to the six directions he carefully placed the first pinch of tobacco into the bowl. With the filling of the pipe the sanctity of the ceremonial area was fully established.

The Flesh Offerings

The three women who had made special offerings in turn walked into the sacred area through an opening in the tobacco string, faced the altar, and held the pipe, with sage, that was proffered them by the *yuwípi* man. Unlike the method of holding the pipe during the sweat bath, the bowl faced the devotee. As a woman would hold the pipe in both hands, stem outward, the *yuwípi* man would cut minute pieces of flesh from her arm with the razor blade. These offerings of flesh were placed in the rattles, the handles having been removed. The blood flowed freely until the *yuwípi* man's assistant wiped the wounds with some sage. The rattles, with handles restored, were returned to their place on the floor. After the ceremony was over I learned that the first woman made this sacrifice for a grandson who had recently been cured and the second woman for a grandson who was in the army overseas. The last woman, the wife of the assistant, had pieces of flesh taken from both arms in thanksgiving (*wóphila*) for her baby, who had survived a long illness.

Those men with drums, the small single-headed variety usually in evidence at these meetings, held them with drumsticks in readiness.[3] The *yuwípi* man was alone in the sacred area, the opening in the tobacco string having been closed, and it was understood that all others would remain seated while the lights were out. On occasion, however, the devotees have been known to dance in place, in the dark.

First Lights-Out Period

The lantern was blown out, after which perfect silence ensued. A tremendous whack on the principal singer's drum signaled the beginning of the singing; the opening phrases of the *yuwípi* songs were as high pitched as possible for the singers. The drumming was purposely discordant, as in the sweat bath, quite unlike the drumming used for dancing songs. The shrilling of the women and children on the closing phrases of each verse was singularly impressive. After constant singing for perhaps fifteen minutes, the lantern was lit. The *yuwípi* had not yet arrived.

The *yuwípi* man announced that he would be tied by his assistant and subsequently released by the *yuwípi* when they arrived on the scene. He also stated that shiny objects might attract lightning and requested me to remove my glasses (wrist watches are usually removed, and mirrors covered, at meetings and during electric storms).

The assistant produced a leather cord and tied the *yuwípi* man's hands and feet while he was standing. He appeared with neither shirt nor shoes when the lamp was lit. The quilt was taken from the pillar and wrapped around him so that even his head was covered, and then more cord was wound around the entire figure, each tied part protected by sage. Amid some muffled grunting he was laid face down on the sage bed with his head toward the altar. After waving the lit sweet-grass rope around the altar and the wrapped figure, the assistant took his seat and picked up his drum. The lantern was blown out.

Second Lights-Out Period

Some piteous moans announced the entrance of the spirits, which the *yuwípi* man named in a muffled voice. *Iktómi* (the Spider), a very powerful spirit, was there; *Ithų́gthąka* (the Rat), *Thaté Oȟ'ą́ko* (Swift Wind), *Čhetą́ Hówašte* (Good-Voiced Hawk), *Wąblí Oȟ'ą́kho* (Swift Eagle), *Phežúta Wakhą́* (Holy Medicine), and *Wąkákįyą* (Flying Above) were all present.

Various noises, such as pounding on the walls, were heard while the devotees sang lustily. The rattles glowed with a blue-green color and began to fly about the room as the *yuwípi* took their offerings of flesh. They struck the four walls, floor, and ceiling, often quite close to the heads of the participants. In this respect both *wašíčhų* were especially favored by the *yuwípi*.

When relative quiet was achieved some of the devotees, in no particular order, addressed the spirits through the *yuwípi* man. Each phrase was addressed to *thųkášila* and answered by muffled grunts or brief comments by the *yuwípi* man. Each of the women who had made sacrifices recited a lengthy account of her troubles. The owner of the house spoke about his sick grandchildren, and I (in English) explained our interest in Lakota religion, which my companion among the singers translated. The medicine man answered that it was "impossible" for us to "learn all about *yuwípi*."

A rhymed prayer by the *yuwípi* man was followed by more singing. One song consisted almost entirely of the typical vocables but contained one important phrase, "*ičímani iyápi*" ("they go on a special trip"). The *yuwípi* would soon leave for the caves, clouds, woods, or water where they reside in order to bring the required power, medicine, or answers to the *yuwípi* man. Their presence continued for a while, as was evident from the noises, moans, and flashing rattles. The drumbeat was changed for another song, not discordant, and then the lantern was lit, revealing the *yuwípi* man completely free of his bonds. The quilt was folded neatly and in its original place on the pillar. The light was quickly extinguished.

Third Lights-Out Period

The *yuwípi* man made some brief remarks, some of which provoked laughter. Several songs were featured during this session. One song was addressed to *Wakhą́ Thą́ka*. Another song, addressed to *thųkášila*, revealed an aspect of Lakota ceremonialism that is quite fascinating; the Lakotas pray for the well-being of the spirits. "Grandfather, I give you this pipe in memory of me. If you do this I will pray for you also." While this song was shrilled to the spirits, Oliver Red Cloud advised us that if we had provided a dog for the feast the pipe would have danced. At many meetings dog meat is the main dish. If it is to be eaten ceremonially, the dog will usually be strangled. The carcass is singed and scraped clean. It is then boiled, often whole if a puppy, with the skin on but the entrails removed.

The rattles flitted violently about amid the pounding and banging on the walls, and then, with a loud swish over the heads of the devotees, the *yuwípi* took their leave. The lantern was lit; the more formal part of the meeting had ended. The *yuwípi* man jested with several persons. One of the singers laughingly revealed that the cord used in tying the shaman was rolled into a tight ball in his jacket pocket. "The *yuwípi* put it there," he said.

After dismantling the altar and the sacred area, the *yuwípi* man returned some of the ceremonial items to his suitcase. The Durham offerings were thrown to the singers and accepted with thanks. One of the women who had addressed *thųkášila* was handed the red cloth that had been tied to one of the sticks. Another woman was given some of the *čhąlí wapháȟta*. Both of these gifts signified that the *yuwípi* would treat their requests favorably. (I know of another occasion when some distraught parents were given a black cloth by the *yuwípi* man. They would soon receive, he informed them, a letter from the War Department advising them that their son was dead.)

The pipe was given to an old woman. She lit it, said "*mithákuye oyás'į*," and after a few puffs passed it to her left. Everyone, including small children, took the pipe and repeated the ceremonial phrase. A chorus of *háu* from the men and *hą́* from the women answered each repetition of the phrase. The pipe was then placed in the suitcase and the feast began.

Plates, cups, and eating utensils were passed clockwise by the girls, men's side first. The meal was typical of traditional Lakotas, consisting of beef soup containing very little meat, store-bought white bread, crackers soaked in warmed tomatoes, and coffee. While the devotees were eating, the students were thanked publicly by the house owner for the feast. No one made any remarks about the absence of dog meat.

The plates were removed, and the assistant passed water clockwise, starting with the men's side. Everyone remained seated as he gave each person a dipperful of water from the bucket he carried. Before or after drinking, all said "*mithákuye oyás'į*" and were answered in the usual manner. With the drinking of the water the ceremony was officially brought to a close. The devotees began to leave, taking their bedrolls, plates, and utensils with them.

The very next day after the Loafer Camp meeting, a Sunday, we experienced events that appropriately illustrate Lakota religious tolerance. All of the male singers, with their families who were present at the meeting, were observed attending mass at Holy Rosary Mission. The same afternoon these people attended a memorial mass at Wounded Knee Chapel, following a feast honoring a deceased Lakota, which was given on the chapel grounds by his family. The singers were quite willing to discuss the previous night's meeting. Later in the summer, two more *yuwípi* meetings were held at the same house, and in late August the house owner performed *hąbléčheya* and provided a big dog-feast after obtaining his vision.

YUWÍPI PAST AND PRESENT

Most Lakota medicine men, particularly the *yuwípi* men, are jacks-of-all-trades, including in their repertoire curing, counseling, finding missing persons or lost articles, predicting, and conjuring. Despite the many stories of trickery told throughout Lakota country, many continue to believe in the power of the *yuwípi* men, ignoring these stories or in some cases simply accepting such phenomena as the noises and flashes as part of the show. I spoke with a young man who was paid by a *yuwípi* man to manipulate the rattles and to rub his fur-covered arms over the faces of the devotees at meetings. The same singers are often used by a variety of medicine men and may themselves be passable conjurers. The older and more experienced practitioners, among them *yuwípi* men, are rather adept at "making the spirits talk" from various points around the room. Often the voices seem to be emanating from the ceiling.

Certain Lakotas have tried to expose the *yuwípi* men as frauds, usually without success. Horn Chips, long dead, can be considered one of those who has greatly added to *yuwípi*'s popularity. For one thing, his spirits spoke in many voices, and all of his prophecies are said to have been fulfilled. Early in this century, by order of the Agency Superintendent who was in charge of Pine Ridge Reservation, Horn Chips' meeting was held in a lighted room. Indian police were present and the police chief himself carefully tied and wrapped the *yuwípi* man. Lights flashed on the ceiling; Horn Chips was no longer tied when the flashing ceased. It is understandable that many Lakotas refer to him as the "real *yuwípi* man." Among his and his brother Moves Camp's descendants are a number of medicine men, both *yuwípi* and those who are not tied and wrapped.

Horn Chips provided Crazy Horse with charms (*wóthawe*) to protect him in battle. This may in part account for the extraordinary numbers of Lakotas who believe that Crazy Horse was an extremely powerful medicine man, which is an extension of the hero worship surrounding this warrior about whom very little is actually known, except for events connected with his surrender in May 1877 and his death while resisting arrest months later.

The *yuwípi* man from Kyle previously quoted has afforded us some singular explanations concerning some of the concepts and practices associated with the ceremony. "The *yuwípi* man," he said, "has to be like a rock, just as Christ said he would build his church upon a rock." This medicine man declared that the earthen mound near the sweat lodge represents the hill upon which Christ fasted, and that sage is used in Lakota ceremonialism since "it is mentioned in the Bible." He further observed that the rattles are used by the *yuwípi* because they do not wish to touch the "sin-filled people." He is one of those Lakotas who equate the *čhąlí waphá̇hta* with a Catholic rosary. When asked why, if *yuwípi* was so Christian in nature, Christian religious articles were removed before the meeting, he declared that he did not remove them. He considered them to be a great aid to his communicating with "the spirits." Another *yuwípi* man, Frank Fools Crow, referred to his pipe as "half a cross" (but when held in an unorthodox manner, vertically, with the prowed bowl above the stem).

Yuwípi, however my friend from Kyle feels, is not to be considered a Christian sect, although still other *yuwípi* men may have very slightly modified their concepts and actions along such lines. I consider *yuwípi* a supremely traditional practice coexisting with the Christian churches and all other features of contemporary Lakota culture. It is so widespread on Pine Ridge and Rosebud that many Lakotas think of darkened-room meetings only in terms of *yuwípi*.[4]

Yuwípi is a welcome vehicle for those seeking spiritual help, relief from the boredom of reservation life, the loneliness, and the frustrations of unsuccessfully attempting to imitate the *wašíčhu*. Even the lukewarm participant, the person who suspects trickery, will applaud a meeting such as that in which the *yuwípi* man was found with his head stuck in a stovepipe. Many Plains tribes are quite familiar with the phenomenon of spirits placing the medicine man in ridiculous situations.

FIVE

OTHER CEREMONIES AND PRACTICES

The most important function of any medicine person among the Lakotas is to cure illness, with or without the benefit of herbs. Various English terms are used by the Lakotas for native practitioners, such as "doctor" and "medicine man." This chapter will be devoted in part to a discussion of the sometimes confusing Lakota designations for medicine men, herbalists, and other religious figures. A description of some of the recent and extant ceremonies, with the exception of peyote, will be included using *yuwípi* as a point of reference. Darkened-room ceremonies conducted by practitioners who are not tied and wrapped are often called *lowápi* or "sings."

NATIVE DESIGNATIONS FOR PRACTITIONERS
Medicine Man.
The English term "medicine man" (or "medicine woman") is used very loosely by the Lakotas, often for the benefit of non-Lakota-speaking persons. Members of all sociological groups on the reservation, including very aged traditionalists, have been known to use this term.[1]

Wičháša Wakhá (Holy Man)
Most Lakotas will apply the term *wičháša wakhá* to any male medicine man. It can also be considered a very loose designation in that it is sometimes used to describe insane persons and berdaches (*wíkte*). Any man who conducts meetings can be called *iyéska* (interpreter), the same term designating mixed-bloods.

Waphíye Wičháša (Doctor Man).

Although often reserved for those Lakotas who practice herbalism without benefit of conjuring during a ceremonial meeting, the term *waphíye wičháša* may be applied to any medicine man.

Phežúta Wičháša (Medicine Man).

The term *phežúta wičháša*, like *waphíye wičháša*, usually refers to those who specialize in or limit their practice to curing with the ceremonial use of herbs. An unusually clear but strictly personal definition was given to me by Melvin Blacksmith, who described a *wičháša wakhą́* as an "all-around holy man" (in terms of power) and a *phežúta wičháša* as a "druggist."

Phežúta Wíyela (Medicine Woman).

The term *phežúta wíyela* is synonymous with *waphíye wíyą* (doctor woman), both designations for female herbalists, who rarely hold ceremonial meetings of their own but often assist men. Some of these women engage in midwifery and prophecy. Invariably these women have reached menopause; menstruating women are considered not only dangerous in themselves but capable of turning any ceremonial rite or meeting into a catastrophe.

Yuwípi Wičháša (Yuwípi Man).

Both the Lakota term and its English equivalent are used in reference to those who specialize in being tied at a ceremonial meeting. Lakotas often use the term *yuwípi* man for any male practitioner. Indeed, in the same conversation a Lakota may describe a ritual specialist as a *yuwípi* man, *phežúta wičháša*, and, in English, a medicine man. When distinguishing between a well-known healer from the Wounded Knee community, who is not tied, and a tied medicine man, a Lakota, when pressed, abandoned the term *yuwípi* man and substituted *waphíye wičháša*. He and the other Lakotas who had entered into the discussion were reminded that the medicine man in question vigorously denied that he had anything to do with *yuwípi*. The consultant was not particularly concerned with the distinction between tied and untied medicine men but was concerned with the spirits or powers they possessed. The Lakotas present based their distinction upon the fact that this untied ritual specialist exclusively possesses eagle power. He is often referred to as an eagle doctor (*wąblí waphíye*), as described below.

It is dubious whether any *yuwípi* man deals specifically with "little people" today. The majority of contemporary *yuwípi* men are released by all sorts of creatures, including toads. There are several untied medicine men who are aided by little people.

Wičháȟmųǧa (Bewitcher)

Anyone who purposely uses his powers to harm others may be termed a *wičháȟmųǧa*. Malevolent medicine men, including those associated with specific ceremonies, poisoners, or those who cast spells and curses, all fall into this category.[2]

The Buffalo-Calf Pipe

The only artifact resembling a tribal medicine bundle known to the entire Lakota people is the *Ptehįcala Čhąnúpa*, the Buffalo-Calf Pipe. *Čhąnúpa* means something used for tobacco and also refers to the act of smoking itself. Some Lakotas sincerely believe that all of their pipes originate with the Calf Pipe.

According to a myth that has been told countless times among the Lakotas and retold in many books and articles, this pipe was given to the Lakotas, specifically the Sans Arcs (Itázipčhos), by the mythical White Buffalo-Calf Woman revered by many Plains tribes. Briefly, the usual version of the story concerns two men who were hunting when their attention was attracted to a beautiful girl dressed in a glowing white garment. One of the men attempted to rape the girl against his companion's wishes. As he touched the virgin he was reduced to a pile of bones, but the man with good intentions was told to prepare his people for her coming. The following day the Calf Woman was received with great solemnity. According to what are probably later versions, along with the pipe she presented to the band she gave instructions for a number of ceremonies, among them the Sun Dance. She then left, transforming herself into a white calf.

Martha Bad Warrior, Itázipčho (Sans Arcs) Lakota, White Buffalo-Calf Pipe Keeper, standing in front of sacred bundle, 1936 (W. A. Riegert photo)

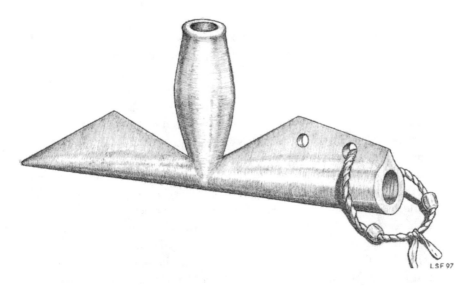

LSF 97

Calf Pipe Bowl, approximately six inches at base with fins undoubtedly much narrowed at top; bead ornaments are of the old blue glass-trade type (after Thomas 1941)

This pipe has been described as having a black, T-shaped bowl decorated with a standing buffalo figure. Others state that it is made from catlinite with the figure of a calf in relief, and still others insist that the pipe is simply an ancient stone tube with an unadorned wooden stem or a femur. In 1936 the pipe was publicly displayed by the keeper, Martha Bad Warrior, a very aged Itázipčho of the Cheyenne River Reservation, who prayed with it to end a devastating drought. It is fashioned of catlinite, and in the mid-1930s it was photographed on two occasions. There is no calf figure (Thomas 1941; Smith 1967).[3]

Among the many persons who have journeyed to see the pipe is John Bear Shield, an Oglála who wished aid and information concerning a sick child. I am not aware of any ceremonial meeting associated with this 1950s unwrapping of the bundle, but Bear Shield was instructed to donate several colored cloths in order to see the pipe, which he described as having a fin (the bowl has two fins). The keeper declared the case to be too far gone.[4]

Lakota Clowns

Lakotas do not consider clowns (*heyókha*) an especially amusing or comical group. In fact, their very presence constitutes a potential danger, particularly at religious functions.

The *heyókha* cannot be considered medicine men as such, for they do not cure, counsel, or find lost articles. What they are capable of is undoing the work of medicine men. In this sense it may be said that clowns are involved with the *wakhą́šiča*, or malevolent powers. I am reminded of the malevolent lamas of Tibet who turn prayer wheels in the opposite direction, thus undoing the merit gained by the orthodox revolutions. The *heyókha* are similar in that they interfere with the natural order and stability of the Lakota ceremonial world by doing things backward. The clowns may emerge from the rear of their tents, often walking backward, and when joining the Omaha dancers will burlesque their activities in ludicrous and ragged costumes (Howard 1954, 257). This contrary behavior amuses the Lakotas until a catastrophe occurs that may be blamed on the clowns. At a very big Omaha Dance on the Pine Ridge Reservation, where hundreds of gaily costumed dancers were prancing and stomping, I noticed two clowns weaving through the group. Joseph Fast Horse, standing nearby, commented on the fine weather and then said, "It's those clowns with mirrors that cause trouble. They can make it thunder and hail." Medicinal herbs are not to be used in the presence of clowns, since the medicine will be rendered useless or harmful.

Clowns may follow the dream and vision sequence much as medicine men do, but apparently they are not usually required to undergo the vision quest. In the dream the candidate may see, in addition to thunder and lightning, himself dressed as a clown, sometimes on horseback. The only regulation to be followed by the *heyókha* is to participate as clowns in Omaha Dances. They are not welcome at the Sun Dance, but there is evidence that some clowns went so far as to burlesque the Sun dancers.[5]

Kermit Bear Shield ignored his original dream until he was threatened by lightning. He "clown dances" in a modernistic costume replete with false nose, derby, hobo clothes, and a whiskey bottle with a nipple but containing no whiskey. Kermit is well liked at the Omaha Dances, where he creates further merriment by throwing eggshells at the spectators. He is very atypical in that he dispenses herbal medicine. He also signed a contract to travel with a carnival. Very contemporary, yes, but it all started with a dream. Another clown seen at reservation functions wore a black hood with a fringed-cloth shirt and leggings. The large hoop he carried completed his traditional costume. On his back, however, was sewn the logo "M and M" for a bar by that name in Martin, South Dakota.

The Horse Dance

A very colorful and impressive ceremony that has fallen into disuse among the Lakotas is the Horse Dance (*Šųgwáči*). One of the primary functions of the Horse Dance is to bring rain. Accordingly, due to the long drought during the early 1940s, a memorable ceremony was held at Oglala, on the Pine Ridge Reservation, involving four groups of four horses, each group comprised of horses of the same color.[6] This very sacred combination, four fours, produced the desired rain and hail, none of which fell in the immediate area. Since that time all subsequent Horse Dances have been unfavorably compared with the affair held at Oglala.

Those who dream of themselves "dancing horses" will be assisted by a medicine man and may accomplish the dictates of their dreams with a minimum of spectators, or may wait for an opportunity such as that presented by a tribal or community fair or dance.

The *Šųgwáči* is also considered a cure for nightmares and various neuroses and psychoses. Rainfall is an expected, immediate result of the ceremony, regardless of what other motive the dancer may have. The horses are to be ridden bareback and unbridled, while the appropriate songs are sung, now known to but a handful of older men. The dancer strips to a breechcloth and moccasins, paints most of his body, and disguises himself with a black cloth hood. A sage circlet is usually worn around his head, and to it may be fastened sacred eagle down or other feathers resembling horns. The horse dancers use eagle-bone whistles, which they blow almost constantly.

During the Sun Dance celebration of 1955 I observed a *Šųgwáči* involving two riders, as described above. Because the ceremony was held in the enclosed

Horse Dance, Pine Ridge, 1955

dancing area and there was a great crowd of spectators, the half-wild horses were bridled. Four women, each bearing a different-colored cloth banner stretched on a short stick and supported by a longer one, preceded the dancers into the shade, and then each stood at a cardinal point. One of the dancers offered a pipe to the sun, the other a small sage hoop. As the singing commenced, the horses were "danced," that is, trotted, to each of the cardinal points and then somewhat wildly ridden around the shade and out of the entrance. The dancers had approached from a point well west of the encampment. Before they disappeared over the rolling plains it rained heavily, the brief storm sending all the spectators running for their cars and tents.

OTHER SPECIALISTS

Many religious ceremonies and practitioners are not in vogue at present on the Pine Ridge and Rosebud Reservations but are remembered and often referred to by persons ranging from the very aged to those in their middle years. Since the Lakotas themselves constantly compare present-day religious practices with those of former days, some of these practitioners and ceremonies of the earlier twentieth century have a place in this discussion.

Mathó waphíye, or bear doctors, have long been known to the Lakotas. They formerly practiced in the Prairie and Woodland areas, where bears were highly revered. The Woodland Ojibwe, to this day, maintain a ceremony to propitiate the spirits of slain bears, which must be performed before any of the meat is consumed. In prereservation times the Lakota bear doctors would don the head and skin of that animal while attempting to cure the sick or injured. They specialized in treating wounds, a function that would cause the warlike Lakotas to regard them with much esteem.

Most older Oglálas and Sičháǧus declare that *mathó waphíye* were numerous until recent times and that *yuwípi* men constitute a new type of healer. One reason for this partially erroneous assumption lies in the fact that most of the medicine men on the reservations today are *yuwípi* men; however, it is quite possible that *yuwípi* men were relatively rare in pre- and early-reservation days, but they are now often equated with traditional religion (Ruby 1955).

A trait universal to bear doctors is that they dug medicinal roots with the aid of a bear claw. They usually performed their magic during a darkened-room or tent meeting featuring prayer cloths and tobacco strings. The grunts of bears were audible throughout the meeting.

The middle-aged grandson of a bear doctor, alluded to earlier, revealed to me that as a child he was fascinated by many of the curious activities of his grandfather. The *mathó waphíye* are to live as bears do, and this doctor obeyed the dictates of his vision in all details. He would, for example, wash himself in a creek every morning by throwing water on himself with pawlike movements, grunting all the while. At present there are probably no *mathó waphíye* among the Lakotas. This does not mean, as will be discussed at the end of this chapter, that such a specialist cannot emerge at any time.

There are still other Lakota medicine men who are untied. Among these doctors is Frank Good Lance, a respected old man with long, braided hair, who resides near Wounded Knee (Feraca 1962). Frank Good Lance is an eagle doctor. He falls into the same category as other doctors who hold ceremonial meetings in which they are assisted by little people, elks, ghosts, or other things *wakháƞ*, but are not tied and refuse to be called *yuwípi* men. Good Lance's meetings are held in the dark. His arrangement of the sacred area is atypical in that he does not have an earthen altar and only three cloths are used (in addition to four smaller red offerings in the central can).[7] A red and a white cloth, each usually on its own staff, are to his right, and a green cloth is on a staff to his left. No reporter has ascertained the symbolism attached to these colors.

Good Lance cures, counsels, and finds lost articles as instructed by the eagles, which enter the room with flitting noises. Sparks and tiny luminescent eagles are seen at Good Lance's meetings. This doctor is peculiar in that he demands only "Indian" food for the feast, such as dog, *wasná* (shredded, dried meat pounded with chokecherries), *wóžapi* (a dessert made with buffalo berries, chokecherries, or other wild fruit), and fried bread.

David Day, mentioned earlier, was noted for treating paralytic cases. This specialist, now deceased, was evidently not a conjurer. Alex Eagle Elk specified that he constructed an altar of ashes in the shape of a crescent and placed cloth offerings at the four corners of the room. *Čhaƞlí wapháȟta* was placed on the altar. The lantern remained lit throughout the ceremony, which is quite an unusual phenomenon. With a rattle and bone whistle the medicine man would call upon *huƞkála* to look after the supplicant, afterward administering various medicines that had been boiled before the ceremony, including the mold from a buffalo-berry bush. At present there are no medicine men devoted to this particular spirit and practice.

Blue Legs, mentioned previously, was a blind medicine man who made use of a powerful catlinite *čhaƞnúƞpa* in communing with the supernatural. This pipe may be considered the nucleus of a medicine bundle and the focal point of a ceremony, since its use constituted the most important element of this medicine man's religious powers. On one occasion, according to the devotees of this ceremony, Blue Legs, praying with the pipe, caused an approaching storm cloud of terrifying proportions to split in two, hail falling on both sides of the party. Blue Legs is fondly remembered for his practice of donating to

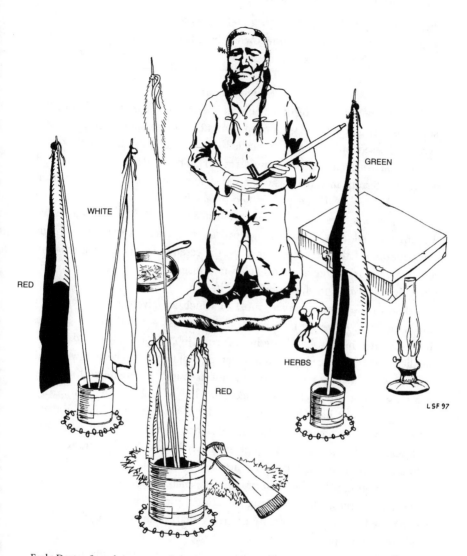

RED

WHITE

GREEN

RED

HERBS

RED

LSF 97

Eagle Doctor Sacred Area, 1959; frying pan contains cedar incense, suitcase contains conjuring aids (after Feraca 1962)

the poor everything given him by grateful persons, even though he lived in absolute poverty. His pipe is now owned by a Lakota family who apparently do not use it for religious purposes.

Sacred Stones

The use of special pipes or other objects *wakhą́* is comparable to that of the small, usually globular or egg-shaped stones that are reputed to possess great power.[8] These stones are properly called *thųką́*, an abbreviation of *thųką́šila*, or *akíčhita* (messengers, the same term for soldiers, derived from the old warrior-fraternity members who conveyed messages and instructions from band authorities to the people). When owned by *yuwípi* men they are often called "*yuwípi* stones," but their function does not differ from those owned by other individuals. The term *íyą wakhą́* (holy stones) is used by many contemporary Lakotas. Whenever a specific ceremonial name for a religious phenomenon is unknown or has fallen into disuse, Lakotas often simply add the adjective *wakhą́* to the name of the item.

Lakotas possess many *thųką́*, most of which are given to the owners by medicine men. A *yuwípi* man gave one to his sister in far-off Los Angeles in order that her husband might secure a job. If properly cared for, as medicine man George Flesh stated (meaning that they are to be kept wrapped, rubbed with fine sage when used, and not used indiscriminately), the stones are powerful in themselves and need not be used in conjunction with a meeting or rite. I have seen a relatively large stone serving as a doorstop. The woman who owned it feared its presence in her house but was afraid to discard it. The stone had been given to her by another woman, who was also afraid to discard it but would not keep it herself. Many older Lakotas will have nothing to do with stone artifacts, such as lance- and arrowheads, believing that these objects belong to various spirits. The Lakotas deny ever having used stone points, firmly asserting that, prior to using metal, they made only bone points.

As we have seen in the description of the Loafer Camp meeting, curing was definitely the primary concern of those present, but counseling and comforting the grandmother of a soldier was one of the *yuwípi* man's duties. Many attempt to find lost articles, which is a practice most often performed by *yuwípi* men. The *yuwípi* locate the articles and report their findings to the medicine man. Many are the tales told by the Oglálas and Sičháǧus concerning the powers of those who have been able to locate missing persons. These stories follow a macabre pattern since the graves, including those of murdered individuals, are found much more often than the living persons. In 1959 a Sičháǧu medicine man was invited to the Yankton Sioux Reservation to locate the body of a white boy who was presumed drowned in the Missouri River. Reportedly he did so. An aged Yankton said, "It was like the devil [operating]."

The Lakotas strongly believe in imminent justice or retribution (*wakhúza*); therefore, many medicine men will not handle cases when it is believed that the afflicted person is being punished for some wrongdoing, such as misusing spiritual power. One medicine man does not ordinarily attempt to find lost articles, since he regards the loss of the articles as some sort of punishment, perhaps for stealing. Related to the Lakota conception of imminent justice is their fatalistic attitude. A medicine man may unemotionally prophesy disaster and make no attempt to avert it, and he may not be expected to do so. However, in keeping with their duties regarding the general good and welfare of the people, it is not unknown for medicine men to attempt to avert tragedy. Violence is very common on the reservations, often directly due to drinking but typically founded upon jealousy, boredom, and the many truly difficult problems of reservation life. The medicine men do not become involved in this sort of thing but are often called upon to deal with such violence. Some Lakotas have stated that those who fear they will kill or maim a personal enemy may be advised to consult a medicine man.

There is little basis for the general assumption, shared by Indians and non-Indians alike, that all religious practices not actually in existence among the Lakotas today are in reality extinct. The term *dormant* seems to be more applicable, in view of the fact that some rites, among them the Sun Dance piercing, have been revived in recent years. Among the many reasons for the emergence of some of these previously dormant practices is the fact that these aspects of Lakota religious life are vivid in the hearts and minds of the people. A Lakota who has never actually seen a bear doctor's performance, to name one ceremony considered dormant rather than extinct, may dream of himself as one of these specialists simply because he has often heard of them.

SIX

PEYOTISM

Most of the publications dealing with peyotism only slightly mention or wholly ignore the Lakotas, the use of the term "Plains" almost invariably referring in these works to such southern tribes as the Kiowas and Comanches. The reason for this omission undoubtedly lies in the fact that the Lakotas were among the last groups to embrace peyotism. The Oglálas and Sičháǧus cannot be considered peyote users like the Kiowas, Comanches, and other societies in Oklahoma and elsewhere. In some of these tribes, where peyotism is strongly entrenched, it may now be said to constitute the tribal religion.

The Native American Church, the very name indicating its affinity with pan-Indianism (Howard 1955), resembled the Ghost Dance in its fairly rapid spread throughout the Great Plains. Like the Ghost Dance it was the bane of federal officials, Christian missionaries, and schoolteachers, and, like the earlier Ghost Dance religious fervor, it also flourished in the face of continued attack from those who were determined to dictate their own religious beliefs to the Indian people.

The Indian people continued the fight until the New Dealers decided that the tribes had a right to worship as they pleased. Prior to 1934, some of the tribes had illegal peyote churches established among them for more than thirty years. With the Collier administration of the New Deal, some groups decided to come out of hiding; others were always defiantly open in maintaining peyotism. The Lakota peyotists have seemingly never been sure of themselves. There is little fanfare associated with peyotism on their reservations. A very few church buildings, for example, are maintained on Pine Ridge and Rosebud. Peyotism has no strength at all on any other Sioux reservations, such as Cheyenne River and Standing Rock.

The Lakota peyotists have long been divided into two sects, Half Moon and Cross Fire, with the latter stronger in terms of membership. These two sects of the church are not separately enumerated under the state charter granted to the Native American Church. This charter, incidentally, like all of the other state charters granted throughout the country, makes no mention whatsoever of peyote. The church can legally hold meetings, but consumption of peyote at these same meetings is illegal, as is transporting peyote through South Dakota. The plant will only grow in certain parts of Texas and northern Mexico. Whites and Indians bootleg it at high prices, and peyote is also sent through the mails.[1]

Both sects, as far as the Lakotas are concerned, incorporate distinctly Christian teachings and practices. Peyote, to the Lakota user, is an instrument of Christianity. The Cross Fire sect uses the Bible at all meetings where sermons are preached, and texts are read in the same manner as at Protestant services. Half Moon does not use the Bible at meetings, but the dogmatic and moral teachings of this sect's leaders are definitely Christian.

An ordinary meeting will begin on a Saturday night and last until sunrise Sunday morning. The Half Moon people build a packed-earth, crescent-shaped altar on the floor of the tent or house where the meeting is to take place. Ashes form the tail of the Water Bird extending below the altar. Both sects construct earthen fireplaces outdoors. Cross Fire received its name from the sect's practice of digging a crossed ditch at the fireplace and then filling the depression with live coals. Each congregation has four ceremonial leaders, the Road Chief, Fire Chief, Drum Chief, and Cedar Chief. The Road Chief, who teaches his followers to "walk the good road" of life, acts as the prayer leader. The Fire Chief starts the cedar fire and replenishes it throughout the ceremony. He is assisted by the Cedar Chief, who sprinkles seeds and needles on the fire or the ashes. The Drum Chief starts the drumming and singing peculiar to the peyote ritual. Only metal water drums are used, the wet skin heads beaten with unwrapped sticks in a very fast, almost unvarying tempo. By tilting the drum or pressing on the edge of the drumhead with the thumb, one can change the pitch several times in the course of a song. The members may bring gourd rattles and feather fans with them. With the rattles they keep time to the single drum.

A Cross Fire meeting commences with the Lord's Prayer. Other prayers may be offered by the members while the peyote buttons and a mash and tea made from them are passed around the room. As the members chew the buttons and mash and drink the tea, the drum throbs continually. Each male who wishes to do so will sing, usually repeating a song four times, or four times four and singing four different songs. The combination of peyote, singing, drumming, rattling, and cedar incense affects everyone in the room or tent. At midnight, with some ceremony, water is passed around the room after the Midnight Water Call is given by the Road Chief. Prayers to the four directions are offered and then the sermon from the Bible is preached. The congregation sings and consumes peyote until dawn, when the Morning Water Call is sung. Soon after, with the Quitting Song, the meeting is ended and a "sacred breakfast" follows, which has been arranged by the promoter.

The Half Moon meeting roughly corresponds to Cross Fire. Few prayers or songs can be considered to belong specifically to the sect; they are primarily personal and individualistic. The Half Moon Road Chief or "peyote man" prays with Durham cigarettes, or sometimes a pipe, but not a Bible.

An outsider observing the artifacts used by both sects will undoubtedly consider them non-Christian at first glance. The beaded and tasseled staff that is passed around the room during the meeting looks traditional but represents Christ's walking staff. The three legs of the single-headed metal drum base represent the Trinity, and the peyote button on the altar is equated with the host in the Christian tabernacle.

The general Lakota term for peyote is *uhčéla* (cactus, and also refers to feather dance bustles that often have two feather spines). Peyote is derived from the Nahuatl word *peyotl*, meaning "caterpillar" (referring to the fuzzy growth on the button), and is usually rendered "peyoti" by most Indians. The Lakotas, however, prefer to say "peyot," with the accent on the last syllable. "Button" and "bean" are other terms employed by the Lakotas, and peyote is often called *phežúta* since it is considered a supremely powerful

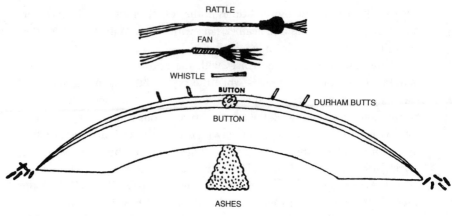

RATTLE

FAN

WHISTLE

BUTTON

BUTTON

DURHAM BUTTS

ASHES

Peyote Altar, Half Moon Rite, top view, 1959 (after Feraca 1963)

medicine by the members. Its use as a panacea is regarded as a major problem by health authorities and many other people who oppose it for nonreligious reasons.

Peyote is the common term for the plant *Lophophora*, which is classified as a single species and the unique member of its genus (La Barre 1938, 10). The more distinct divisions merely classify the plant as to age and potency: *Lophophora williamsii* is the more mature plant containing nine alkaloids, and *Lophophora lewinii* is the younger plant containing only one alkaloid (La Barre 1938, 138–50). Often called a "mescal button," this term has led to the erroneous assumption that the buttons are derived from the mescal plant. The active ingredient of the drug produced by *Lophophora*, however, is called mescaline. The tribes in this country and Canada use only the round, fuzzy, buttonlike portion of the plant, the only part visible above ground.

The Kiowas and Comanches became avowed peyote ritualists soon after their reservation life began in Oklahoma. These two tribes are to be regarded as the early diffusers of peyote in the plains, employing proselytizing methods to influence other tribes. The Lakotas present many divergent accounts of just which tribesmen brought the ritual to their country. Those who accepted it and learned the ritual became peyote leaders, without usually experiencing dreams and traditional vision quests. The Lakotas believe that the effects of the plant were discovered by two Southwest Indians of an unspecified tribe who were lost in the desert. After eating several plants in desperation, the button of the peyote plant was found not only to allay hunger and thirst but to produce the pleasurable drugged effect. They supposedly introduced the plant to their own tribe, where the ritual connected with its use was established. Some tribes in northern Mexico were ancient peyotists.

Peyotism was received by the Oglálas and Sičhą́ǧus sometime between 1910 and 1915 and is therefore relatively late among them, other tribes having established strong churches before 1900. No one tribe is credited with diffusing it to the Lakotas, but the Northern Arapahoes and the Nebraska Winnebagos are both largely responsible, with the latter group probably exerting more influence than the former. Many Christian songs originally composed by the Winnebagos are reportedly translated into Lakota. The Arapahoe songs are sung in the original and composed entirely of vocables.

It has been very difficult to determine the frequency of meetings and the number of bona fide peyote members on the two reservations under consideration here. Suffice it to say that meetings are held only sporadically, "every Saturday night" being evidently nothing more than wishful thinking. The occurrence of a meeting is primarily dependent on the availability of a promoter or the peyote itself.

Peyote users can be found in all parts of the reservations, but certain locales are considered peyote areas. Porcupine, Wounded Knee, and Allen are strong peyote areas on Pine Ridge, whereas Soldier Creek and places near St. Francis have heavy peyote-using populations on Rosebud. Few peyotists are listed as such on official rolls as far as religious preference is concerned. The practice of being listed as Roman Catholic, Episcopalian, or Presbyterian, and yet having little to do with these churches, is common. As the spread of peyotism among the Lakotas is fairly recent, many of its adherents were not members by birth. In addition, it is consistent with Lakota tolerance for one to worship with several congregations during the course of a year. To further confuse the situation, there exists the practice of considering oneself a member of a parent's congregation, but having little or no intercourse with that same congregation. When first visiting the reservations I was much amused by the comment made by a woman who was Protestant, her husband Catholic. "He and the boys are Catholic," she said, "and me and the girls are Protestant. We divvy up." While she was thus discoursing her husband was singing "spirit songs" addressed to *Wakhą́ta*, an abbreviated form of *Wakhą́ Tháka*. "They're real pretty," she observed.

My estimate that 10 percent of those who might be considered traditional Oglálas are peyote members should be taken with caution. Possibly the same percentage of the Sičhą́ǧus are peyotists. Hurt, however, considers these estimates much too generous (Hurt 1960b, 22).

The attitudes of the nonusers among the Lakotas toward members range from bitter condemnation to tolerance and amusement. Some speak of the meetings as "dope parties" and the like. Many of the Lakota critics do not think the peyotists serious about their faith because of their often perfunctory manner (though this is typically Lakota) of attending to the business of the church. It is pointed out that in Oklahoma peyote is a "real religion" and the members "dress up to go to church," whereas the Lakotas hold meetings at their leisure (which is not true) and in ordinary attire. Peyote is indeed marginal, unlike *yuwípi* and other traditional Lakota ceremonies previously discussed. Nonusers never wholly deny traditional religious power, although many Lakotas, including some very aged people, declare that all such power disappeared with the introduction of Christianity. Peyote is not a traditional form of Lakota worship, and peyote leaders are not considered powerful in themselves. I know of a Half Moon peyote man who requested that a darkened-room meeting be performed on his behalf by a traditional medicine man. The Half Moon leader had been ill for a long period, and evidently the peyote was not effective. It is not unknown for a traditional medicine man to function also as a leader in a peyote congregation.

The term *member*, rather than *devotee*, has been applied to the peyotists since the Cross Fire sect practices baptism (an initiation), both sects (at least ideally) hold planned meetings, and there is complete and open intercourse between the leaders and their fellow adherents. Nonmembers consider the combination of drum, rattles, and Bible to be quite incongruous, but *yuwípi* devotees and others involved in such rites see nothing untoward in using tomato cans as ceremonial artifacts, in equating a Sun Dance pole with a cross, and in persisting in their reverence for Christian images. Some of the Christian elements found in the versions of the peyote ritual are distinctly Roman Catholic. I received an explanation of the Trinity from a Sičháǧu Half Moon leader that revealed far more knowledge of this aspect of Catholicism than can be boasted by many practicing Catholics.

The story of one unfortunate peyote man is told amid much hilarity by the Oglála nonmembers. This leader, dressed in white robes and bearing a decorated staff, was unceremoniously bucked off the mule he was riding while in the presence of a group of anxious members. Such attire, combined with the staff and mule, clearly reveals the intensity—if only on the surface—of the Lakota peyotists' desire to equate the ritual with Christianity. To use a Christian analogy, the Cross Fire people can be considered "fundamentalist" in their views and practices.

In the summer of 1954 a very large but unadvertised Native American Church convocation was held in the Porcupine district on Pine Ridge. Another convocation, under the auspices of the Episcopal Church, was held at the same time elsewhere on the reservation. Similar outdoor revival meetings within tent encampments are held by other churches, and the intention of rivalry seems clear on the part of the peyotists. By most estimates the 1954 peyote meeting, which lasted several days, attracted the larger number of participants. During Holy Week, and to a certain extent during Christmas Week, peyote meetings are held throughout the reservations. For several days prior to Easter 1958, a large peyote meeting was held right in Pine Ridge village, to the great annoyance of the rest of the residents. The police finally asked the peyotists to leave. They complied and resumed their meeting out in the country. *Yuwípi* and other traditional meetings are rarely held during Christmas and Holy Week, and they are not held on Sundays.

Despite all the Christian traits of the peyote ritual, some real and some quite superficial, Catholic and Protestant clergy deny the existence of anything that can be termed "Christian" peyote. In 1954 a prominent Jesuit long associated with the Lakotas said, "There is no such thing as Christian peyot" (employing the Lakota pronunciation). He further observed, "People who are divorced or in bad marriages have to go somewhere, so they go to peyot."[2] The members are sometimes buried in cemeteries belonging to their local peyote congregations. Most of the graves are marked with simple white crosses.

Although experiments have proved mescaline to be non–habit forming, and in this sense not a narcotic, the early view that it is persists today in many otherwise well-informed circles. The fact that mescaline acts as a temporary drug is unchallenged, and if one prefers to use the expression "intoxicated" in referring to those under the effects of mescaline, most authorities will condone this usage. However, as responses to the various arguments against peyote, these considerations are of dubious value. The Lakota nonmembers often speak of peyote and heroin in the same breath, although they may have never experienced either. Pronounced alcoholic intoxication is often equated with the effects of peyote.

The accusation that the use of peyote aggravates the omnipresent problem of alcoholism among the various Plains tribes seems to be quite unfounded. The attitude of peyote members—and this applies to all tribes—is that the desire for liquor is satisfied by consuming peyote or that the moral teachings of the church effectively discourage drinking. Others are of the opinion that peyote is a substitute for alcohol since it not only produces intoxication but usually has much less of an aftereffect. Although I am in no position to adopt one argument or the other, it can be stated that many Lakota and Nebraska Winnebago nonmembers have declared that significant numbers of persons in their tribes have become teetotalers after joining the church. Whether such a change is due to moral teachings, psychological reasons, the actual influence of mescaline, or a combination of all these cannot be determined here.

Against the accusation that peyote consumption leads to disorderly conduct and fighting, it can be argued that many individuals have terminated their pugilistic tendencies after becoming peyotists. Again, many nonmembers share this view and point to friends and relatives who have embraced peyotism and become nonaggressive. One of the teachings warns that if a formerly wayward person lapses into his old way of life while a member, the peyote itself will cause great suffering, which is identical to the belief, called *wakhų́za* (as mentioned earlier), about abusing or misusing things *wakhą́*. Disagreeable visions experienced at meetings are usually interpreted as warnings to desist from evil ways. The Lakota peyote songs are often addressed to Jesus, who is asked to forgive sin and help the member to live a moral life. During the meetings it is deemed mandatory that a member fix his attention upon some worthy thoughts. Members are often accused of sexual perversion and the meetings described as orgies. This is entirely unfounded, as the meetings are quite orderly in every respect. Among the Lakotas the disorderly element can be attributed to young nonmembers who force their way into the meeting places, thus precipitating a fight for which the members will be blamed. Nonmembers are often surprised to find the peyotists so friendly and docile while a meeting is in progress.

Medical and hygienic issues present the only important bone of contention between peyotists and authorities, both non-Indian and Indian, who are informed and tolerant in their views. Peyotline is a good sedative, but the other alkaloids contain no useful properties. In view of this information most of the "cures" reported by members are without medicinal basis. The members, however, present an endless list of "hopeless cases" that are supposedly cured by peyote. (The devotees of medicine men's practices and traditional herbalism present much the same list in discrediting the efforts of *wašíčhu* medicine men and medicines.) Peyote is used as a treatment for everything from the common cold to tuberculosis. I doubt its medicinal value in the treatment of any stomach disorder, since the very bitter buttons invariably produce some gastritis. Peyote is often used to attempt to cure dysentery, which afflicts young and old on Pine Ridge and Rosebud. It does not seem logical, in view of the gastritis produced by even small quantities of peyote, that it can cure dysentery. It is more probable that it only adds to the problem. Some adherents compare peyote with barbiturates, but it is more accurate to say that wakefulness is the result of a meeting. This has been my experience.

Probably the most heated and confusing controversy concerning the use of peyote is centered around the accusation that a large proportion of users are insane. Nonmembers in all tribes are generally convinced that consumption of large quantities over a long period of time will end in insanity. On the other hand, users are emphatic in their claims that the drug is an excellent and speedy cure for nervousness and insanity. Experiments along these lines have been attempted, but the unstable nature of mescaline prevents it from being of any real aid to mental health. Nervousness, exaggeration of all reflexes, and wakefulness are the immediate effects of meetings, as I can attest. It follows that the more frequently one attends meetings the more pronounced these symptoms may become, and may plague the member even outside the meetings.

Many Lakotas will chew and swallow at least ten buttons during a meeting; those without teeth drink large quantities of tea. Some members regularly consume over two dozen buttons at a meeting and partake of peyote outside of meetings, perhaps daily. It seems quite probable that such overdoses could result in nervous disorders. A Jesuit priest, who had spent many years with the Oglálas, stated that frequent users became psychotic due to the action of the drug upon the pupils of the eyes, causing objects to appear out of proportion or gigantic. He further believed that most of the Lakota mental patients in the area's hospitals were peyote users. This claim can be generally discounted, but the observation about impaired vision is corroborated by others.

Lakotas have given me their opinions about a young Sičháǧu believed to be insane as a direct result of consuming peyote. The man in question was definitely psychotic and a devoted member. He died in the summer of 1954 in a South Dakota state mental hospital and was buried with honors by his local Half Moon congregation, which held the wake meeting typically following the death of one of its members. William Blue Horse, the peyote man who arranged for this meeting on Grass Mountain near St. Francis, and the other members of the congregation were quite saddened by this young man's demise. He is reported to have been extremely likable and quite sane before involving himself with peyote. He suffered from delusions of nonexistent monetary wealth, and at one time terrified the occupants of a bus by accusing innocent people of stealing his horses.

The feeling of well-being is fondly recalled by Lakotas and others who have attended one or more meetings merely out of curiosity. At the first meeting I attended, with a Half Moon congregation, I eventually realized that everyone else seated in the large, rectangular tent structure had their eyes closed. At first perplexed, I followed suit and immediately experienced technicolor visions of grids intertwining with and separating from each other; these were followed by even more colorful, Disney-like parrots. Later I reflected on my genuine surprise at having any particular association with parrots and such peculiar geometric forms. Another nonmember, speaking of the rapid beating upon the water drum, stated that he felt as if he were being lifted up and down to the tempo. The same person recalled that all forms of music sounded extremely pleasurable to him for the remainder of the day (as they did to me). He said, however, that he was not forced to consume peyote while witnessing the meeting. This attitude is generally shared by the members and is consistent with their rather tolerant manner of proselytizing.

There is an attitude to be found among many Lakota nonmembers that the peyotists are shiftless and uninhibited. They often blame the high automobile-accident rate on peyote users, but the ruinous state of the cars and alcoholism are usually at fault. The alkaloid peyotline produces aversion to all physical and mental effort. This fact may justify the accusation that some peyotists are shiftless, but only in terms of how often and how much peyote is consumed. An elementary school teacher formerly of Pine Ridge reported that the slovenly habits of some pupils can be attributed to the use of peyote. He cited the example of children who are given peyote tea for breakfast when food is lacking in the home. They remained listless for the entire morning at school, often fixing their unwavering gaze at some spot on the blackboard.

Earlier predictions of the demise of peyotism have proved entirely false. The former missionary fervor of the members has, however, practically disappeared in favor of recruitment among the children of peyotists. The Native American Church was a forerunner of pan-Indianism. Many people undoubtedly join it simply because it is formed and directed by members of their own tribe, a new member often being related to the local leader. The use of the vernacular, that is, the tribal language, the nature of the ceremonial rites and artifacts, and the incorporation of Christian elements all combine to make the church an "Indian" religion. For the conscience-stricken Christian there is the Bible; for those who find goodness in traditionalism there are the drum and rattle. Add to these attractions the peyote itself, and we have a combination that explains peyotism's popularity.

SEVEN

HERBALISM

It was hot inside Emma Smoke's frame house in Porcupine. That afternoon in August 1956 the bedridden old woman was feeling worse than usual. She had been almost completely paralyzed for several years with a severe arthritic condition, although her gnarled, stiffened fingers could still produce excellent beadwork. Mrs. Smoke had tried many forms of medical assistance, including visits to the Pine Ridge hospital, in an effort to alleviate her condition. *Yuwípi* meetings, and those of related practitioners, had frequently been held for Mrs. Smoke and her psychotic daughter, who died in a sanitarium. Her passing worsened her mother's condition.

Besides myself and the herbalist who arrived later, only female relatives of Mrs. Smoke were present. The sister, daughters, and granddaughters who hovered around the old woman were all traditional, but the granddaughters were rather "modern minded." In very weak tones Mrs. Smoke asked for someone to summon a herbalist who lived nearby. Mrs. Smoke's daughter, Lizzy, immediately arose from her seat on the couch alongside her mother. The other daughter produced her husband's pipe, an L-shaped, catlinite bowl with a simple wooden stem. Lizzy wordlessly accepted the pipe, which was kept in a cloth case with the stem attached to the bowl.[1] Her niece accompanied her on the short drive to the herbalist's home. In less than fifteen minutes the two emissaries returned with the pipe and the *waphíye wíyą*, Mrs. George White Bull, a very diminutive, aged lady, who was seen Sun dancing later that month.

Lizzy began to boil water on a kerosene stove. The *waphíye wíyą*, bearing the medicine in a soiled rag sack, sat down near Mrs. Smoke and inquired about her condition, which was apparently aggravated by lack of sleep and digestive disorders. Mrs. Smoke replied briefly and paid the herbalist two dollars. The medicine consisted of dried roots, flowers, and leaves. *Ičáȟpe hú* ("rubs against root"), also known as purple coneflower (*Echinacea angustifolia* or *Brauneria angustifolia*) or white snakeroot (*Eupatorium rugosum*), is considered the most powerful ingredient (Buechel 1970, 200). Several noxious weeds that produce rashes when rubbed against the skin share the appellation *ičáȟpe hú*, poison ivy being one of these. The herbalist put about a handful of the mixture into the water and boiled it for a few minutes. No prayers or songs accompanied this treatment. Mrs. Smoke drank some of the tea, which was given to her in a cup by the herbalist. The patient's dress was opened while the herbalist held some of the tea in her mouth and then spat on the chest, abdomen, and neck. She then blew on these same areas and slightly massaged them. The treatment lasted less than three minutes.

After the herbalist left, Mrs. Smoke complained to her sister, Mrs. Mary Fast Horse, that the medicine was very bitter (which it was). She compared the taste with peyote tea, which she had tried outside of meetings, having a strong aversion to peyotism. At irregular intervals the local Episcopal catechist would visit her and conduct a hymn and Bible service in her house, assisted by other members of the family. One such service was held a few days after the herbalist's visit.

Mrs. Fast Horse is well versed in the gathering of medicines and their various properties. She and her husband had been given the power by medicine men to gather and use several kinds of plants. They were instructed, that is, in the rites associated with these medicines, a basic aspect of "going for medicine," since all medicines belong to the supernatural beings. Some Lakotas assert that mounted figures in human guise will often advise a medicine seeker about the danger of certain plants. These figures who ride through the heavens are newer powers adopted by the equestrian Lakotas. They exist side by side with the older, winged spirits like *Wakíyą*, who owns many medicines. Mrs. Fast Horse's husband was severely injured in an automobile accident that left him a cripple until his death. Since he was virtually bedridden, his wife was

Mary Fast Horse (1888–1970), Oglála Lakota Herbalist, wearing beaded buckskin dress and women's breastplate, 1960

requested to seek medicine that he, but not his wife, had the power to gather. She finally found the courage to gather this specific plant that did not belong to her. Four days later one of her colts was struck by lightning. Nearby flashes of lightning or the presence of snakes are interpreted as warnings not to pick or dig the plant that is being sought. With Mrs. Fast Horse's guidance we will describe in detail the gathering of two herbs she often used.

GATHERING *PHEŽÚTA PHÁ*

Blue Legs gave Mrs. Fast Horse the power to use *phežúta phá* and instructed her in the appropriate songs and prayers and the placing of the offerings. *Phežúta phá* simply means "bitter medicine" and is made from the dried leaves and flowers of the golden prairie clover (*Parosela aurea*). She explained that it is easily distinguished by its white flower and grows, to her knowledge, in only one place on the reservation, near the old Number Four day school in Payabya community on Pine Ridge. Since I asked for a sample of the medicine, she requested a dollar to purchase the necessary offerings. In a general store she bought six strips of cotton cloth a few inches wide and about a foot and a half long and four sacks of Durham. Each cloth was of a different color in accordance with the symbolism described below.

A song is to be sung the night before *phežúta phá* is gathered. Since she and I were riding with some friends in the vicinity of the school and had the tobacco and cloth with us, she decided to look for the plant and then sing the appropriate song. Such a decision, based on practicality, is typical of Lakota unorthodoxy. I was directed to cut and peel six chokecherry wands no more than a foot long, while she left the car and searched for the medicine. None could be found, an obvious disappointment since she wanted to replenish the small supply she had gathered previously. She decided to give me some of what she had, the same rites applying as in actually gathering the plant. On the way home she explained that *phežúta phá*, mixed with *ičáȟpe hú*, was good for a variety of ailments, particularly kidney, liver, and venereal diseases.

A few days later, at my suggestion, preparations were made to approach the spiritual powers associated with the plant. That night, in her house, Mrs.

Fast Horse sang the following prayer-song, without drum or rattle accompaniment. The words given below were only slightly embellished with vocables. Each of the six stanzas of the song, associated with a particular category of spirits, was sung once. The first stanza is given in its entirety.

Wiyúȟpeya etą́hą
Thųką́ eyá šá ya'ų́pi
Hó uwáyįkte namáȟ'ų ye.

At the west
You grandfathers who are red are there
I will raise my voice and you hear me.

The second stanza refers to the north (moving clockwise), and the color symbol is white. The third is for the east (yellow); the fourth refers to the south (black). The fifth stanza addresses *wąkátuya thųką́*, the heavenly grandfathers, who are blue, and the sixth and last stanza is sung for *makhátąhą thųką́*, the earthly grandfathers, who are gray. Unlike most other rites, in this case the red represents the west and the sunset, white the north and snow, yellow the east and sunrise, black the south and the hot winds of death, blue the heavens and the winged spirits *Wąblí Gleška* (the spotted or mature golden eagle) and *Wakį́yą*, and gray the earth itself.

The following morning a pinch of tobacco from one of the Durham sacks was tied in a corner of each cloth, and each cloth was tied to a stick with the same cotton string. Mrs. Fast Horse stated that a stick was not necessary for the gray cloth since it is placed right on the ground (a stick was used, however). The banners were not hanging loose in the more typical fashion but tightly wrapped around the sticks. Late that afternoon, while lightning was flashing, but in the distance, the cloth offerings and Durham were placed in a paper bag and carried to a hill in sight of the house. Such offerings are rarely placed near the house for fear of lightning. In this instance she wished to walk even farther, but a storm was threatening.

Upon selecting a spot on the grassy hillside Mrs. Fast Horse placed the bag on the ground and began to pray. As she held her bowed head in one hand, she said she would pray to Jesus; "That's the first one." "*Até Wakhą́ Tȟą́ka*" ("God the Father," a Christian form) and "*ničhį́kši* Jesus" ("your son Jesus") were mentioned in the prayer. It was asked that, on my behalf, the "soldier who was to suffer hardships" and the "young man who desired medicine" be recognized and pitied. The pleas "pity me," "pity us," and "pity him" were often voiced, as they are in all traditional Lakota prayers. One must appear pitiful to approach the powers. Thunder and lightning spirits were requested to send rain for the good of the grass and wild fruits, such as chokecherries. The entire prayer was said in Lakota but ended with the biblical "Amen."

She then took the cloth offerings from the bag and held each one in turn as she faced the appropriate direction and repeated the words to the song sung the previous night. Each wand was pushed into the ground as the stanza was completed except the last wand, the gray one, which was placed on the ground. The four sacks of Durham, replete with papers, were then removed from the bag, which was unceremoniously thrown away. Holding the Durham in both hands, Mrs. Fast Horse said a prayer to *Wąblí Gleška* and *Wakíyą*, asking their permission to use the medicine and also requesting that strong hail, strong winds, and other perverse elements not prevail. The Durham sacks were then placed on the ground amid the cloths. She stated that the Durham sacks must remain for at least one night, after which anyone could take them for smoking. The light was fading and thunder was ominously rolling. She resolved to move the offerings the next day. Two days later she dug *ičáȟpe hú* and moved the offerings. Rain prevented these activities from being completed sooner.

We ascended the treeless hill and found the Durham sacks intact, but at first glance it appeared that the cloth offerings were gone. Mrs. Fast Horse was elated at this, believing that when she was praying she had felt the presence of the "holy things" and that they had taken the offerings. A closer search revealed them to be some distance away and not too far apart except for the wand with the white cloth. She was rather pleased by the fact that the white cloth had been carried far, about twenty yards. The scattering of the others she attributed to rain and wind. All the cloth offerings were removed and taken farther from the house. They were placed not in but on the ground under a pine tree, where they were to be found by the spirits. The Durham offerings were not removed from their original position.

DIGGING *IČÁĤPE HÚ*

As mentioned previously, *ičáĥpe* means "rubs against," and *hú* in this instance means the root of a plant with a white or pinkish, daisylike flower, which grows abundantly in the plains. Evidently only the root is used, *ičáĥpe hú* being a very common traditional Lakota medicine, whether taken alone or with other herbs.

Mrs. Fast Horse dug the root with a stick, taking great care not to break it. When the root was freed a pinch of tobacco was broken off a cigarette, and she said a prayer to *Wąblí Gleška*. The usual pleas for pity were made, and the "soldier who desired medicine" was mentioned. The tobacco was placed in the cavity, the plant stem replaced, and the earth pressed in to keep the stem and flower erect. One more root was dug, but the tobacco offering and prayer were omitted, this being necessary only in digging the first root of a day's gathering. The stems, however, are always replaced. The long, thin roots were washed and cut into small segments to be mixed with the *phežúta phá*, which Mrs. Fast Horse kept with other dried medicines in a tin container. A jar of the flower, leaf, and root mixture was given to me. When actually used this mixture is to be boiled twice, the second time in a different pot. It is taken as tea and also placed on the ailing part of the body. Another prayer to spirits, addressed as grandfathers, is said when the mixture is put into the boiling water and again when the medicine is being taken by the patient.

According to Mrs. Fast Horse, practically every flowering plant and bush in the area has a medicinal use or property. This does not mean, of course, that anyone may gather and make use of them. She pointed out various plants as buffalo, elk, and bear medicine, but she had never gathered them. She has a small supply of very minute seeds to be used in treating venereal disease and other urinary ailments. These seeds grow near Mrs. Smoke's house in Porcupine. Another medicine in her possession is a root known as *phežúta hutékhą* (simply "medicine root"). It had been administered to her daughter for "kidney trouble." Mrs. Fast Horse administers cedar-seed tea for dysentery and digestive complaints. To gather the seeds, she prayed and left tobacco and a dime at the base of the tree.

Most Lakotas, including many young people, sincerely believe that, other than trauma and some stomach and eye disorders, there were no serious ailments afflicting Indians of prereservation days. This may be attributed in part to the mythology of the supposed primordial paradise formerly enjoyed by all Indians.

There are many reasons why the Lakotas still attempt to cure their ailments with traditional ceremonies and remedies. Among these is the real fear that most traditional people have of being alone and away from their immediate families. The government hospitals, formerly administered by the Bureau of Indian Affairs and now by the Public Health Service, maintain clinics that are fairly popular with the people. However, no traditional Lakota wishes to be confined to the hospital itself, and many persons in need of prolonged medical care will not visit the clinic for fear of being remanded to the hospital. An Oglála woman with a severe heart condition, which finally killed her, said, "I'd rather use Indian medicine than go to the hospital. If you go in there they never let you out." The Indian Health Service people are not in an enviable position. Arrayed against them are medicine men, herbalists, individuals with grudges against the clinics and hospitals, and an old heritage that does not admit of germs or patience with healers.[2]

The position of some health authorities concerning native practitioners is that they no longer constitute a threat to government health programs. We have seen that this is by no means true. Should the medicine men and herbalists pass from the scene—which does not seem likely in the near future—native concepts concerning the causes of illness and the treatment to be administered would still persist. The traditional people are willing to undergo treatment from white doctors (*wašíčhų wakhą́*) only insofar as their own concepts of medicine are not denied or disturbed. Prolonged treatments, especially in the hospital, are anathema to them. Relatives of hospital patients have been known to bring peyote and other native medicines with them on visits. The Lakotas, particularly younger patients, are notorious for leaving the hospital without a release. The medicine men may constitute a relatively small threat in themselves, but the power concept and miserable socioeconomic and sociopsychological conditions remain formidable obstacles facing the health authorities. I believe that many individuals like Mrs. Fast Horse wield more influence, through numbers alone, over more people than the medicine men and professional herbalists (such as Mrs. White Bull).

In the 1950s I received a letter from someone very close to me, an Oglála who believed that he was going blind and stated that the Pine Ridge hospital could do nothing for him. I wrote to the hospital officials and received a reply in which it was suggested that I strongly urge this man to go back to the hospital and present a detailed medical history, which he had not done previously. Dr. Lewis Patrie, the medical officer in charge who kindly replied to my query, wrote:

> One of our problems with the people on the reservation is the difference in concept of physician between the health personnel and the patients. Sometimes I feel that the Indian people expect somewhat of a supernatural healer who diagnoses just by being in the presence of a patient rather than by a thorough history, examination and whatever necessary laboratory tests are indicated. If you could emphasize the concept of a physician as you understand it in the United States culture, this might also help Mr. ———— ———— to accept medical care.

Hypochondria, or at least the serious exaggeration of symptoms, is omnipresent on the reservations. I was once awakened by a distraught mother, who asked that her daughter be taken immediately to the hospital in my car. She believed that her daughter had a "bursting bladder" and "bleeding kidneys." I quickly handed her husband the car keys and the girl was sped away to the hospital. The very next day she was released since it appeared that menstruation was all that afflicted her. It is fascinating to learn about the myriad "hopeless cases" that have been cured by medicine men, herbalists, or others who administer native treatments and medicines. A Lakota stated that an eye infection that threatened to blind him was pronounced hopeless by the hospital physicians. A *phežúta wíyela*, he asserts, sucked at the swollen eye until a foreign object was removed. Sucking out malevolent spirits or real causes of bodily infection was practiced aboriginally. Many of the stone and clay tubes found at archaeological sites were used not for smoking but for sucking from the bodies of the sick either stones or tiny arrowheads that appeared magically or intangible causes of disease.

An account concerning the noted Black Elk should serve to illustrate just how difficult it can be for the Lakotas to distinguish between the power concept and what is useful and practical in treating the sick. He was called upon to cure a woman well known to me who had been bitten by a rattlesnake. After tightly tying a string on the leg above the bite, he chewed a root, which he placed on the bite. The string was then removed and a line painted around the leg; Black Elk explained that the string was no longer needed.[3]

The germ "theory," of course long since accepted as fact in modern medicine, is virtually unknown to many Lakotas. A dozen persons sleeping in one or two rooms is a common practice. Drinking from the same dipper and eating from plates that have been badly washed are still everyday features of reservation life. The swarms of flies around homes and encampments in spring and summer are merely regarded as a nuisance. The schoolchildren are generally unaware that flies cause such racking illnesses as dysentery. In the summer the Lakotas accept dysentery as part of the business of living.[4]

CONCLUSION

The Lakotas are a tolerant and adaptable people. There has never been any real strife among the various Christian denominations, but in this respect inter- and intrafamilial strife is not unknown. They attend and often participate in each other's services with ease and enjoyment, at the same time considering themselves members of a particular church. All Lakotas think of themselves as at least nominally Christian, yet the vitality of the traditional power concept remains. The people who attend two masses the day following a *yuwípi* meeting are not extraordinary in their tolerance. Representations of Christ and the Virgin that are usually removed from rooms being prepared for meetings are immediately replaced at the conclusion of the meetings. At least one medicine man considers these religious items to be of great assistance to him in conducting his version of the *yuwípi* meeting. In many traditional prayers and songs the Christian Deity is invoked along with animal spirits and thunder and lightning beings. No Lakota, however, would equate *Wakíyą* with *Wakhą́ Thą́ka* any more than a Christian missionary would consider the angel Gabriel equal to the Savior.

Yuwípi has been reintroduced to Lakota tribes other than the Oglálas and Sičhą́ǧus. *Yuwípi* men have appeared among the Northern Tetons of Cheyenne River as a direct result of the frequent visits to their reservation by Oglála and Sičhą́ǧu practitioners. It is also possible that *yuwípi* will be brought to non-Sioux Plains tribes who may have once been familiar with tied conjurers. Reportedly, the Oglálas have introduced it to the Northern Arapahoes.

Peyotism is not to be considered essentially a traditional Lakota phenomenon, and although a forerunner of pan-Indianism it seems to have become relatively stabilized in contrast to its former rapid growth. To the Lakota peyotists, it represents a satisfactory combination of traditional and Christian elements, but peyotists from other tribes familiar with less of a Christian atmosphere at their meetings will nevertheless feel at home while visiting the Lakotas. The externals of the ceremony are much the same from Arizona to Saskatchewan; the effects of consuming the button do not vary with geographical location. The Lakota users who find themselves among tribes that conduct a non-Christian peyote meeting are quite capable of singing Christian songs at such a meeting.

Medicine men per se are not wholly essential to the continued existence of some ceremonies and most beliefs and practices now in vogue among the Lakotas, such as the Sun Dance and the gathering of herbs for medicine. The Sun Dance held on Pine Ridge in 1956 was directed by the principal dancer, since no medicine man would assume the responsibility. The ceremony would probably have been satisfactory were it not for the rain that began hardly an hour after the dancing commenced. Two days later, during the social or Omaha dancing, a few Sun dancers attempted to intrude. It began raining as they entered the lodge; the Lakotas knew why. Herbalists, both male and female, who hold no ceremonial meetings abound on the reservations as they do in white, black, and Hispanic communities throughout the country. Of course, the Lakotas differ in regarding herbs as sacred and the property of spiritual powers.

The unveiling of trickery in the darkened-room meetings usually disgraces the specialist but rarely disgraces the belief. At Rosebud some worthy turned the light on, revealing the medicine man standing with his eyes closed while manipulating noise makers. He left the reservation in disgrace. At a *yuwípi* meeting at Pine Ridge a man grabbed a rattle that flitted close to him in the dark. He was denounced as an unbeliever and told that he would be struck by lightning the following summer. The Oglálas recall with amusement that although the *yuwípi* man has long been dead, the mischief-maker is still living.

A factor of much importance to the continued existence of night meetings and certain other Lakota ceremonies is the conservatism of the old people. We must realize, however, that the old people were not always old, and there will always be old people. The aged Lakota of today was supposed to have become, according to many predictions that have proven entirely false, a self-supporting, completely acculturated farmer or rancher. He is no such thing, and neither are those of his grandchildren who have lately taken an interest in things Indian and may not wait to reach middle age before dabbling in ceremonialism.

With the progression of time since the early 1960s it has become quite evident that while some may be "dabbling," significant numbers indeed do not await their middle years before embracing what they regard as Lakota traditional religious practices. These developments, generally removed from Christianity and supported by the larger society, thrive in an atmosphere of New Nativism and New Ageism.

I am currently working on a synthesis of the truly voluminous writing on Lakota religion since the 1960s; a description and analysis of the current situation with particular attention to innovation, invented tradition, New Nativism, and New Ageism influencing and influenced by the Lakotas; and the attendant national and international involvement of Lakotas, non-Lakota Indians, and non-Indians.

By the 1990s, in contrast with the earlier scene as described in the text of this monograph, there has emerged what one colleague has characterized as an "explosion" of interest and involvement in Lakota religion. The young Lakotas who began participating in the 1960s are now at least in their fifties and in many instances have become mentors. Those who near the close of this century are in their teens and early adulthood, again in contrast with former years, are participating in a very public atmosphere virtually devoid of the constraints known to their ancestors. It is now very apparent that almost any practice can make its reappearance but may do so with novel features that reconstitute tradition.

In writing the original conclusion to this work, I was admittedly cautious. I am now even more cautious about making a statement about whether the combination of traditional fear, respect, and propriety, so basic to the observance of Lakota religion, will be maintained as the people enter a new century.

NOTES

PREFACE

1. The only term that does not follow accepted orthographic conventions is *Lakota*, which retains the traditional spelling throughout this book. Otherwise, I have observed the conventions established by David Rood and Allan Taylor in *Languages*, volume 17 of the *Handbook of North American Indians* (Washington DC: Smithsonian Institution, 1996). I have, however, retained the traditional spelling of *Wakinyan* in the title, for ease of reference in bibliographic searches; throughout the rest of the book I use *Wakįyą*.

1. A BRIEF HISTORY OF THE LAKOTAS

1. "Sioux" is a now unpopular designation that is, nevertheless, wholly unavoidable in studying the historical background of the Lakota and other Sioux people. A detailed account of Lakota migrations, Plains settlement, and the early agency period is found in Hyde 1950, 1957, and 1961. For prereservation history, White 1978 and Anderson 1980 are excellent sources. For political, territorial, and cultural divisions of the Sioux, see Feraca and Howard 1963 and Howard 1966. In the latter works the term *Nakota* is employed, about which some scholars understandably express concern. The "Nakotas" or "Middle Dakotas" — meaning the Yanktons and Yanktonais — call themselves and their dialect "Dakota," but they are aware that they differ from the Santees or Eastern Sioux, the Dakotas proper.

2. The Húkpaphas, Mnikhówožus (Miniconjus), Itázipčhos (Sans Arcs), Sihásapas (Blackfeet Sioux), and O'óhenųpas (Two Kettles). The other Sičhą́ǧus are known as Lower Brulés or Kulwíčhašas.

3. By anthropological reckoning, the Buffalo-Calf pipe (see chapter 5), for example,

may be Arikara or Mandan in origin (Smith 1967, 28–29). The Lakotas attribute much of their religion — and this belief has been strongly reasserted since the 1960s — to the acquisition of this pipe.

4. For all practical — and indeed very important — purposes, there were only two treaties that affected the Lakotas (and the Yanktonais), those of 17 September 1851 and 29 April 1868. The latter superseded the former. The Sioux remain unaware that the Treaty of 1868 does not contain a single viable provision, which is very pertinent to religious matters, especially Sioux attitudes regarding the Black Hills. Concerning controversies over these treaties and the Black Hills mythology, see Feraca (1990, chaps. 2 and 3), which is based on material drawn primarily from an assignment at the Bureau of Indian Affairs to develop recommendations regarding the beneficiary tribes to the Black Hills claim award and the division of the funds among them.

5. The chapel was burned to the ground the day after the end of the occupation by armed, militant Indians in 1973. To this day, the perpetrators remain officially unknown.

6. Like the internationally known Black Elk, baptized Nicolaus by a German Jesuit.

7. Since the 1960s many clergymen, particularly Catholic, have become more than tolerant of traditional religion. Church attendance, however, is generally poorer than in the 1950s and early 1960s, and church marriages are becoming even more of a rarity. Since the 1960s a number of Lakotas are being married by medicine men, which is purely the result of New Nativism. Such practitioners did not — contrary to Hollywood mythology — conduct weddings in any Indian tribes.

8. In the 1990s the Lakota people date such permissiveness to the American Indian Religious Freedom Act of 11 August 1978 (*Statutes at Large* 1978, 92, 469). They have, in fact, forgotten these aspects of the New Deal days (see Feraca 1990, 216–18).

2. THE SUN DANCE

1. American Horse later complained to a white visitor that the singers were taking entirely too long to change from one Sun Dance song to another. Most Lakotas insist that there are seven songs but that the singers in the 1950s and early 1960s had forgotten two of them. In 1974 I heard a Sun Dance song without words, unquestionably of the pre- or early-reservation style, delivered by a single older

Oglála. I have never heard this particular song sung in public, and this individual never sang for the ceremony.

2. Since the 1960s the Lakotas have introduced the dance to societies as geographically and culturally distant from them as the Navajos, Northern Paiutes, and a Tri-Racial group in Maryland. Lakota Sun Dances in the 1990s involve large numbers of young people, including non-Sioux Indians, whites, Hispanics, blacks, and still others, including Chinese and Japanese.

3. This revived the piercing that to my knowledge has become a basic aspect of every Lakota Sun Dance and similar ceremonies among the Yankton Sioux and the Assiniboines. Since the late 1960s virtually all male dancers are pierced, which was not the case in pre- and early-reservation years. Again, see Feraca 1990, 216–18.

4. In the 1990s, in a given dance the participants may face the four directions, the pole, circle the pole, and dance toward and away from it in different "rounds" or dancing periods.

5. Lakota Sun Dances in the 1990s are held for four days, which is a recent development and, contrary to popular belief, unknown in pre- and early-reservation days insofar as the dance itself was concerned.

6. From the late 1950s into the 1970s the Oglala Sioux Tribal Council sponsored and directed the entire celebration. One year, the council truly offended the tribal members by actually charging them admission to the Sun Dance itself. The huge tribal Sun Dance encampment on Pine Ridge no longer exists. At least since the 1970s, Sun Dances have been directed by a variety of leaders or "chiefs" in various parts of the reservations, as many as three dances being held at one time. Encampments, however, are sometimes very small and spectators few in number.

7. In the 1990s the shade is called an "arbor" or "bower."

8. At my prompting, in 1961 a virgin, the director's granddaughter, delivered the first four ceremonial cuts with an ax. The tree was caressed and prayed over by the director and the dancers before being cut by the girl and then felled by her father.

9. For native illustrations see J. O. Dorsey 1894 and Densmore 1918.

10. Black, red, yellow, and white banners have been considered indispensable for the pole since the 1960s, and have appeared in great profusion in the 1990s, as in the "Bear Shield Dance" (named for the leader) in 1996.

11. Not until after the initial publication of this work did I understand that for the

Lakotas the brush bundle represents a sacrifice to insure an abundance of wild plant foods. In 1967 a most knowledgeable consultant, Eugene Wounded Horse, stated that plum branches were to be included with the chokecherry shoots because "that's what they eat." Ideally, the shoots or boughs are supposed to include at least unripened fruit. He made no mention of a nest. In 1996 this concept was affirmed, but one Sun Dance leader not too firmly asserted that the association was with a bundle of arrows that a warrior in prereservation times tied to the pole. It is known that offerings of arrows were sometimes included in the bundle. The Lakotas, however, like all other Plains tribes that place a brush bundle on the pole, arrange the shoots or branches as in an eagle's nest, that creature's habits being closest to those of *Wakįyą*. An exception is found in a painting, whose whereabouts are now unknown, of a Sun Dance by a Lakota artist. The bundle resembles a horizontal bouquet with all the cut or butt ends of the shoots to one side. In every other instance known, including old native drawings, leafy ends appear at both sides. Since the emergence of New Nativist concepts, which in this instance include the influence of elements in Black Elk's now famous visions (Neihardt 1932), the Sun Dance "pole" has become a whole cottonwood tree in full leaf. In the 1990s, the day before dancing commences is known as "tree day," when the tree is felled, decorated, and erected. The brush bundle, as a result, is no longer prominent as part of a cross and is not meant to convey so Christian a notion. What might have been the nest of a mythical being became part of a Christian symbol but always also represented a plea for food, and remains, in appearance, unquestionably a nest.

12. Since the piercing of 1961 and increasingly thereafter, this attitude has definitely changed as far as the younger Lakotas are concerned. In the 1990s, nevertheless, many Lakotas have little respect for the ceremony as now conducted, and therefore they do not attend, citing what they regard to be many abuses.

13. The dance form itself is in the 1990s not nearly so demanding, nor is the use of whistles. Dancers have adopted a loose style, including a side-to-side, shoulder/arm movement. The singing, correspondingly, more resembles powwow music and does not lend itself to dancing in a stiff, vertical position and whistling in time to the beat. Some dancers do not have whistles; others only intermittently use them.

14. The desire to impress a member of the opposite sex is quite possible as a motive, including for non-Indians, in the 1990s.

15. I should now admit that I used a length of wire, but as directed by the dancer, to secure the brush bundle. The rain that made a failure of this ceremony (wire being metal and therefore totally inappropriate) was blamed by some Lakotas on this innocent student.

16. In the 1990s at least two Oglála Sun Dance leaders will not permit the presence of whites as either dancers or spectators. What is done about those who call themselves Indians remains problematic.

3. THE VISION QUEST

1. The term "lamenting," as employed for the vision quest in the Black Elk account (Neihardt 1932), is a poor translation, lending itself to confusion with, for example, grief associated with the loss of a relative. The actual wailing and crying, however, may be quite similar.

2. By the 1990s this situation had very perceptibly changed, young Lakotas making public their aspirations in this regard and their expected acquisition of spiritual power or at least a feeling of well-being.

3. In the 1990s the vision quest, for an astounding number of Lakotas, other Indians, and non-Indians, is often a group exercise with participants in calling distance of each other at favored places on the reservations, at Bear Butte at the edge of the Black Hills and Devils Tower in Wyoming.

4. In the 1990s women subject themselves to long periods, four days being the standard for both sexes. Emphasis is placed as much on the length of suffering as on the goal of a vision.

5. In the last three decades (that is, up through the 1990s), witchcraft and misuse and abuse, deliberate and otherwise, have become matters of great concern on the reservations.

6. It has already appeared in print (dedication in Feraca 1990) that this so highly respected and kind woman adopted me as her son (in 1954). A truly traditional person, she passed away in 1970. At the risk of seeming trite (but this is of great importance in any attempt to assess the quality of traditional religion in the nineties), it should be said that the people of her generation who dressed and thought and expressed themselves as they did are no more. Of great relevance is the fact that the young, with few exceptions, cannot speak Lakota.

4. YUWÍPI

1. This chapter closely follows an old article (Feraca 1961). *Yuwípi*, the practice of tying and wrapping the medicine man, had been very briefly mentioned, but not so designated, by Frances Densmore in her work on Standing Rock Reservation early in this century (Densmore 1918, 218, 235, 246). *Yuwípi* had also been described by Hurt and Howard (1952), Hurt (1960a), and Ruby, a Pine Ridge physician (1955), who includes a valuable photograph of specialist George Plenty Wolf with his ceremonial area and altar. Still other and more recent sources appear in the suggestions for further reading.

2. Usually, *yuwípi* men and other specialists use four small red strips in the central can. They insist that the reference is to the four directions, although only one color is evident. Each of the other cans contains a different color. In the pre- and early-reservation period only red cloth offerings were made, regardless of the direction. Sticks with small buckskin pouches of tobacco were the very old offerings and were stuck in the earth outdoors or in tipis. Since the 1960s, the colors black, red, yellow, and white have also been associated with the human "races."

3. Almost without exception, the Lakotas call these "*yuwípi* drums," even if used in other kinds of night meetings, and they are apparently unaware that these were virtually the only types of Plains drums known prior to the adoption of large, double-headed drums, usually beaten by several singers for dances. In very old days a buffalo hide was stretched by wooden stakes to make a Sun Dance drum (Bad Heart Bull 1967, 95). The wooden water drum and the flat double-headed drum of the Prairie or Woodlands have been entirely forgotten.

4. True *yuwípi* specialists are rare in the 1990s, but growing numbers of younger men, untied, are practicing as medicine men. If not actually conducting meetings, they are officiating at sweat ceremonies or as Sun Dance leaders. Catholic clergy have been making extraordinary statements about traditional religion being an approach to, but not an actual fulfillment of, Christianity.

5. OTHER CEREMONIES AND PRACTICES

1. Since the 1960s the English designations "holy man," "spiritual leader," "spiritual advisor," and "mentor" have been commonly employed.

2. In 1996 Lakotas expressed genuine fear about this aspect of religious life to me, in stark contrast to the atmosphere of the 1950s and early 1960s.

3. The pipe is currently kept by a member, Arvol Looking Horse, of the same family that has had custody for generations on Cheyenne River at Green Grass Village, where many Lakotas have journeyed to ask favors of it through the keeper. The pipe, together with other articles and the cloth and skins that wrap it, constitutes a medicine bundle (*wašíčhų*). This bundle is revered for its own power by many Lakotas who hold sacred the ancient religious concepts, including those in the 1990s who reject the medicine men.

4. It was rare for the bundle to be opened for an individual request and is practically inconceivable in the nineties, but recently the wrapped bundle has been displayed.

5. In 1996, at Parmelee on Rosebud, two clowns taunted Sun dancers with water and cigarettes.

6. A reproduction of a painting by W. Langdon Kihn of this Horse Dance appears in the July 1944 issue of *National Geographic*.

7. Fugle maintains that since Good Lance did not use stones in his ceremony, he did not construct an earthen altar (Fugle 1966, 8). However, such an altar is not directly associated with stones. For example, the earthen altar of the old Sun Dance (revived at Pine Ridge in 1960) and still others for various ceremonies were not made to accommodate stones. Most practitioners do make earthen altars and do use stones.

8. For photographs of typical *thųká*, see Densmore 1918 (plates 29 and 30).

6. PEYOTISM

1. For Indian people, the legal status of peyotism has been much clarified by the amendments to the Indian Religious Freedom Act of 1978, these found in the Act of 6 October 1994 (*Statutes at Large* 1994, 108, 3127). Predictably, a problem persists in defining an Indian, since many legally constituted tribes, including the Oglala and Rosebud Sioux, have nothing resembling current, official membership roles. Of concern also are non-Indians who have genuinely converted to or adopted peyotism.

2. Since the 1960s these views have changed insofar as some clergy, particularly Catholic clergy, are concerned.

7. HERBALISM

1. The injunction to "break" the pipe when not in use, meaning to keep the bowl and stem separate, made its appearance in the 1960s, the rationale being that a pipe is so powerful that leaving it intact should be avoided. Previously, I had neither heard nor read of this practice nor seen evidence of it, including in regard to the pipes of aged medicine men. Powers (1977, 86) apparently accepts this as an old proscription.

2. Lest anything I have said imply otherwise, I wish to emphasize that I highly respect the physicians and other health and sanitation personnel and remain very grateful for the cooperation of the Indian Health Service during the period in which I was engaged in community development on Pine Ridge.

3. Black Elk has become an American cult figure, but this was the only time he was mentioned during my residence among the Lakotas in the 1950s and early 1960s. During at least the last three decades Lakota religion, indeed "Indian" religion, has been equated with this man's "teachings."

4. While it is true that many Lakotas in the 1990s have dwellings, and facilities, that are the result of a variety of housing programs, most remain overcrowded and in disrepair. Factors that all too frequently contribute to poor health, like poor diet, drug and alcohol addiction, and difficult interpersonal relations, continue to be extremely threatening.

SUGGESTIONS FOR FURTHER READING

HISTORY

Anderson, Gary C. 1980. "Early Dakota Migration and Intertribal War: A Revision." *Western Historical Quarterly* 11, no. 1: 17–36.

Anderson, Harry. 1956. "An Investigation of the Early Bands of the Saone Group of Teton Sioux." *Journal of the Washington Academy of Sciences* 46: 87–94.

Church Missions. 1914. *A Handbook of the Church's Missions to the Indians.* Hartford: Church Mission Publishing.

Dakota Presbytery Council. 1886. *The First Fifty Years: Dakota Presbytery to 1890* with *Dakota Mission Past and Present, A.D. 1886.* Minneapolis: Tribune Job Print Co. Reprint, Freeman SD: Pine Hill Press, 1984.

Danker, Donald F. 1981. "The Wounded Knee Interviews of Eli S. Ricker." *Nebraska History* 62, no. 2: 151–243.

DeMallie, Raymond J. 1982. "The Lakota Ghost Dance: An Ethnohistorical Account." *Pacific Historical Review* 51: 385–405.

Digmann, P. Florentine, S.J. 1922. "History of St. Francis Mission 1886–1922." Manuscript. Archives of Saint Francis Mission, Saint Francis SD.

Duratschek, Claudia, O.S.B. 1947. *Crusading along Sioux Trails: A History of the Catholic Indian Missions of South Dakota.* Yankton SD: Grail.

Fritz, Henry E. 1959–60. "The Making of Grant's Peace Policy." *Chronicles of Oklahoma,* 37, no. 4: 411–32.

―――. 1963. *The Movement for Indian Assimilation, 1860–1890.* Philadelphia: University of Pennsylvania Press.

Goldfrank, Esther S. 1943. "Historic Change and Social Character: A Study of the Teton Dakota." *American Anthropologist* 45: 67–83.

Howard, James H. 1960. *Dakota Winter Counts as a Source of Plains History.* Anthropological Papers, no. 61. Bureau of American Ethnology, bulletin 173. Washington DC: Smithsonian Institution. 335–416.

———. 1968. *The Warrior Who Killed Custer: The Personal Narrative of Chief Joseph White Bull.* Lincoln: University of Nebraska Press.

Howe, M. A. DeWolfe. 1911. *The Life and Labors of Bishop Hare: Apostle to the Sioux.* New York: Sturgis and Walton.

Hyde, George E. 1957. *Red Cloud's Folk: A History of the Oglala Sioux Indians.* New ed. 1937. Norman: University of Oklahoma Press.

———. 1956. *A Sioux Chronicle.* Norman: University of Oklahoma Press.

———. 1961. *Spotted Tail's Folk: A History of the Brule Sioux.* Norman: University of Oklahoma Press.

Lazarus, Edward. 1991. *Black Hills/White Justice.* New York: HarperCollins.

Mattes, Merrill J. 1960. "The Enigma of Wounded Knee." *Plains Anthropologist* 5, no. 9: 1–11.

McGregor, James H. 1940. *The Wounded Knee Massacre from the Viewpoint of the Sioux.* Baltimore: Wirth Brothers.

Miller, David Humphreys. 1959. *Ghost Dance.* New York: Duell, Sloan, and Pearce.

Mooney, James. 1896. *The Ghost Dance Religion and the Sioux Outbreak of 1890.* Smithsonian Institution, Bureau of American Ethnology, Annual Report 14, pt. 2. Reprint, Lincoln: University of Nebraska Press, 1991.

Olson, James C. 1965. *Red Cloud and the Sioux Problem.* Lincoln: University of Nebraska Press.

Overholt, Thomas. 1974. "The Ghost Dance of 1890 and the Nature of the Prophetic Process." *Ethnohistory* 21, no. 1: 37–63.

Prucha, Francis Paul, S.J. 1976. *American Indian Policy in Crisis: Christian Reformers and the Indian, 1865–1900.* Norman: University of Oklahoma Press.

———. 1979. *The Churches and the Indian Schools, 1888–1912.* Lincoln: University of Nebraska Press.

Rahill, Peter. 1953. *Catholic Indian Missions and Grant's Peace Policy.* Washington DC: Catholic University Press.

Riggs, Stephen R. 1869. *Tah-koo Wah-kan; or, The Gospel among the Dakotas.* Boston: Congregational Publishing Society.

————. 1887. *Mary and I: Forty Years with the Sioux*. Enlarged ed. Boston: Congregational Sunday-School and Publishing Society.

Robinson, Doane. 1904. *A History of the Dakota or Sioux Indians*. South Dakota Historical Collections, Pierre SD, vol. 2. Reprint, Minneapolis: Ross and Haynes, 1967.

Sisters of Saint Francis. 1886. "Notes from Saint Francis Mission, 1886." Saint Francis Mission Papers, Marquette University Archives, Milwaukee WI.

Sneve, Virginia Driving Hawk. 1977. *That They May Have Life: The Episcopal Church in South Dakota, 1859–1976*. New York: Seabury Press.

Stephan, J. A. 1895. *The Bureau of Catholic Indian Missions, 1874 to 1895*. Washington DC: Church News Publishing.

Tyler, S. Lyman. 1963. *A History of Indian Policy*. Washington DC: U.S. Department of the Interior.

Utley, Robert M. 1963. *The Last Days of the Sioux Nation*. New Haven: Yale University Press.

————. 1993. *The Lance and the Shield: The Life and Times of Sitting Bull*. New York: Henry Holt and Co.

Vestal, Stanley. 1957. *Sitting Bull: Champion of the Sioux*. New ed. 1932. Norman: University of Oklahoma Press.

Wehrkamp, Tim. 1978. "Manuscript Sources in Sioux Indian History." *South Dakota History* 8, no. 2: 143–56.

Westropp, Henry, S.J. 1908. "Catechist among the Sioux." *Catholic Missions* 2: 113–15.

White, Richard. 1978. "The Winning of the West: The Expansion of the Western Sioux in the Eighteenth and Nineteenth Centuries." *The Journal of American History* 65, no. 2: 319–43.

GENERAL CULTURE AND RELIGION

Bad Heart Bull, Amos. 1967. *A Pictographic History of the Oglala Sioux*. Ed. Helen H. Blish. Lincoln: University of Nebraska Press.

Beckwith, Martha Warren. 1930. "Mythology of the Oglala Dakota." *Journal of American Folklore* 43: 339–42.

Brown, Joseph Epes, recorder and ed. 1971. *The Sacred Pipe: Black Elk's Account of the*

Seven Rites of the Oglala Sioux. New York: Penguin Books. New ed., 1953. Norman: University of Oklahoma Press.

Buechel, Eugene, S.J. 1970. *A Dictionary of the Teton Dakota Sioux Language: Lakota-English, English-Lakota.* Ed. Paul Manhart, S.J. Pine Ridge SD: Red Cloud Indian School; Vermillion SD: University of South Dakota.

————. 1978. *Lakota Tales and Texts.* Ed. Paul Manhart, S.J. Pine Ridge SD: Lakota Language and Cultural Center.

Bushotter, George. 1887–88. "Lakota Texts with Interlinear English Translations by James Owen Dorsey." Manuscript. National Anthropological Archives. Washington DC: Smithsonian Institution.

Curtis, Edward S. 1908. *The North American Indian.* Vol. 3. New ed. New York: Johnson Reprint Corporation.

Deloria, Ella C. 1932. *Dakota Texts.* Publications of the American Ethnological Society, vol. 14. New York: G. E. Stechert & Co.

————. [1937?]. "Old Dakota Legends." MS30x8a.21, Boas Collection, American Philosophical Society Library, Philadelphia.

————. 1944. *Speaking of Indians.* New York: Friendship Press.

DeMallie, Raymond J. 1978. "George Bushotter: The First Lakota Ethnographer." In *American Indian Intellectuals,* ed. Margot Liberty. St. Paul: West Publishing. 91–102.

————. 1984. *The Sixth Grandfather: Black Elk's Teachings Given to John G. Neihardt.* Lincoln: University of Nebraska Press.

DeMallie, Raymond J, and Robert H. Lavenda. 1977. "Wakan: Plains Siouan Concepts of Power." In *The Anthropology of Power: Ethnographic Studies from Asia, Oceania and the New World,* ed. Richard Adams and Raymond D. Fogelson. New York: Academic Press. 154–66.

DeMallie, Raymond J., and Douglas R. Parks, eds. 1987. *Sioux Indian Religion: Tradition and Innovation.* Norman: University of Oklahoma Press.

Densmore, Frances. 1918. *Teton Sioux Music and Culture.* Smithsonian Institution, Bureau of American Ethnology, bulletin 61. Reprint, Lincoln: University of Nebraska Press, 1992.

Ewers, John C. 1955. *The Horse in Blackfoot Indian Culture, with Comparative Material from Other Western Tribes.* Bureau of American Ethnology, bulletin 159. Reprints:

St. Clair Shores MI: Scholarly Press, 1977; Washington DC: Smithsonian Institution Press, 1980.

Feraca, Stephen E. 1963. *Wakinyan: Contemporary Teton Dakota Religion*. Studies in Plains Anthropology and History, no. 2. Browning MT: Museum of the Plains Indian.

———. 1966. "The Political Status of the Early Bands and Modern Communities of the Oglala Dakota." W. H. Over Museum, University of South Dakota, *Museum News* 27: 1–26.

———. 1990. *Why Don't They Give Them Guns? The Great American Indian Myth*. Lanham MD: University Press of America.

Feraca, Stephen E., and James H. Howard. 1963. "The Identity and Demography of the Dakota or Sioux Tribe." *Plains Anthropologist* 8, no. 20: 80–84.

Hassrick, Royal B. 1964. *The Sioux: Life and Customs of a Warrior Society*. Norman: University of Oklahoma Press.

Howard, James H. 1955. "Pan Indian Culture of Oklahoma." *Scientific Monthly* 18, no. 5: 215–20.

———. 1960. "The Cultural Position of the Dakota: A Reassessment." In *Essays in the Science of Culture in Honor of Leslie A. White*. Gertrude E. Dole and Robert L. Carneiro, eds. New York: Thomas Y. Crowell Co. 249–58.

———. 1966. "The Dakota or Sioux Tribe: A Study in Human Ecology." Anthropological Papers, no. 2, W. H. Over Museum, University of South Dakota, *Museum News* 27, nos. 5–10.

Laubin, Reginald, and Gladys Laubin. 1977. *Indian Dances of North America: Their Importance to Indian Life*. Norman: University of Oklahoma Press.

Lewis, Thomas H. 1980. "The Changing Practice of the Oglala Medicine Man." *Plains Anthropologist* 25: 265–67.

Lynd, James W. 1864. "The Religion of the Dakotas." 2nd ed. 1881. *Minnesota Historical Collections* 2: 150–74.

Malan, Vernon D., and Clinton Jesser. 1959. "The Dakota Indian Religion." Rural Sociology Department, South Dakota State College, bulletin 473.

Macgregor, Gordon. 1946. *Warriors without Weapons: A Study of the Society and Personality Development of the Pine Ridge Sioux*. Chicago: University of Chicago Press.

Mekeel, H. Scudder. 1931. "Field Notes, Summer of 1931, White Clay District, Pine

Ridge Reservation, South Dakota." Archives of the Department of Anthropology, American Museum of Natural History, New York.

Melody, Michael Edward. 1978. "Maka's Story: A Study of Lakota Cosmogony." *Journal of American Folklore* 91: 149–67.

Neihardt, John G. 1932. *Black Elk Speaks: Being the Life Story of a Holy Man of the Ogalala Sioux.* New York: William Morrow and Co. Reprints: Lincoln: University of Nebraska Press, 1961, 1979; New York: Pocket Books, 1972.

Nurge, Ethel, ed. 1970. *The Modern Sioux: Social Systems and Reservation Culture.* Lincoln: University of Nebraska Press.

Powers, William K. 1977. *Oglala Religion.* Lincoln: University of Nebraska Press.

Riggs, Stephen R. 1893. *Dakota Grammar, Texts, and Ethnography.* Vol. 9 of *Contributions to North American Ethnology,* ed. J. Owen Dorsey. Washington DC: Government Printing Office.

Rood, David S., and Allan R. Taylor. 1996. "Sketch of Lakhota, a Siouan Language." In *Languages,* ed. Ives Goddard. Vol. 17 of *Handbook of North American Indians,* ed. William Sturtevant. Washington DC: Smithsonian Institution. 440–82.

Ruby, Robert H. 1955. *The Oglala Sioux.* New York: Vantage Press.

Steinmetz, Paul B., S.J. 1969. "Explanation of the Sacred Pipe as a Prayer Instrument." Indian Health Service, *Pine Ridge Research Bulletin* no. 10: 20–25.

———. 1970. "The Relationship between Plains Indian Religion and Christianity: A Priest's Viewpoint." *Plains Anthropologist* 15: 83–86.

———. 1990. *Pipe, Bible, and Peyote among the Oglala Lakota: A Study in Religious Identity.* Stockholm Studies in Comparative Religion 19. Almquist and Waksell, Revised ed.: 1980. Knoxville: University of Tennessee Press.

———. 1984. *Meditations with Native Americans: Lakota Spirituality.* Santa Fe NM: Bear and Co.

Walker, James R. 1980. *Lakota Belief and Ritual.* Ed. Raymond J. DeMallie and Elaine A. Jahner. Lincoln: University of Nebraska Press.

———. 1982. *Lakota Society.* Ed. Raymond J. DeMallie. Lincoln: University of Nebraska Press.

———. 1983. *Lakota Myth.* Ed. Raymond J. DeMallie and Elaine A. Jahner. Lincoln: University of Nebraska Press.

White, Robert A. 1974. "Value Themes of the Native American Tribalistic Movement among the South Dakota Sioux." *Current Anthropologist* 15, no. 3: 284–89.

Wissler, Clark. 1907. "Some Dakota Myths." *Journal of American Folklore* 20: 121–31, 195–206.

———. 1912. *Societies and Ceremonial Associations in the Oglala Division of the Teton-Dakota.* Anthropological Papers, vol. 11, pt. 1. American Museum of Natural History. New York: The Trustees. 1–99.

THE SUN DANCE

Deloria, Ella C. 1929. "The Sun Dance of the Oglala Sioux." *Journal of American Folklore* 42: 354–413.

Densmore, Frances. 1920. "The Sun Dance of the Teton Sioux." *Nature* 104, no. 2618: 437–40.

Dorsey, George A. 1905. *The Cheyenne.* 2 vols. Anthropological Series 9, nos. 1, 2. Publications 99, 103. Chicago: Field Columbian Museum. Reprints: New York: Kraus Reprinting Co.; Glorieta NM: Rio Grande Press, 1971.

Dorsey, James O. 1972. *A Study of Siouan Cults.* Bureau of American Ethnology, Smithsonian Institution, annual report 11, 351–544. New ed.: Seattle: Shorey Book Store.

Feraca, Stephen E. 1957. "The Contemporary Teton Sioux Sun Dance." Master's thesis, Columbia University.

Fletcher, Alice C. 1883. "The Sun Dance of the Ogalalla Sioux." *Proceedings of the American Association for the Advancement of Science* 31: 580–84.

Franks, Kenny A., ed. 1976. "The Sun Dance of the Sioux." Written and illustrated by Frederick Remington. *South Dakota History* 6: 421–32. Reprint of Frederick Schwatka, *The Sun Dance of the Sioux* (New York: Century Publishing Co., 1889–90).

Holler, Clyde. 1995. *Black Elk's Religion: The Sun Dance and Lakota Catholicism.* Syracuse: Syracuse University Press.

Hultkrantz, Ake. 1980. "The Development of the Plains Indian Sun Dance." In *Perennitas: Studi in Onore di Angelo Brelich.* Roma: Edizioni dell'Ateneo. 223–43.

Jorgenson, Joseph G. 1972. *The Sun Dance Religion* [Shoshone and Ute]. Chicago: University of Chicago Press.

Karol, Joseph S., S.J., ed. 1969. *Red Horse Owner's Winter Count*. Martin SD: Booster Publishing Company.

Lewis, Thomas H. 1972. "The Oglala Teton Dakota Sun Dance: Vicissitudes of Its Structures and Functions." *Plains Anthropologist* 17: 44–49.

Liberty, Margot. 1968. "A Priest's Account of the Cheyenne Sun Dance." W. H. Over Museum, University of South Dakota, *Museum News* 29, nos. 1–2: 1–25.

Mails, Thomas E. 1978. *Sundancing at Rosebud and Pine Ridge*. Augustana College, Sioux Falls SD: Center for Western Studies.

Mails, Thomas E., assisted by Dallas Chief Eagle. 1979. *Fools Crow*. New York: Doubleday & Co. Reprint, Lincoln: University of Nebraska Press, 1990.

Medicine, Beatrice. 1981. "Native American Resistance to Integration: Contemporary Confrontations and Religious Revitalization." *Plains Anthropologist* 26: 277–86.

Melody, Michael Edward. 1976. "The Lakota Sun Dance: A Composite View and Analysis." *South Dakota History* 6: 433–55.

Nurge, Ethel. 1966. "The Sioux Sun Dance in 1962." *Proceedings of the XXXVI Congreso Internacional de Americanistas*, Seville, Spain, 1964. Seville: ECESA. 3: 102–14.

Paige, Darcy. 1979. "George W. Hill's Account of the Sioux Indian Sun Dance of 1866." *Plains Anthropologist* 25: 99–112.

Schlesier, Karl. 1990. "Rethinking the Midewiwin and the Plains Ceremonial Called the Sun Dance." *Plains Anthropologist* 35, no. 127: 1–27.

Skinner, Alanson. 1919. *Notes on the Sun Dance of the Sisseton Dakota*. Anthropological Papers, vol. 16, pt. 4. American Museum of Natural History. New York: The Trustees. 381–85.

Spier, Leslie. 1921. *The Sun Dance of the Plains Indians: Its Development and Diffusion*. Anthropological Papers, vol. 16, pt. 7. American Museum of Natural History. New York: The Trustees. 450–527.

Walker, James R. 1917. *The Sun Dance and Other Ceremonies of the Oglala Division of the Teton Dakota*. Anthropological Papers, vol. 16, pt. 2. American Museum of Natural History. New York: The Trustees. 50–221.

Webb, H. G. 1894. "The Dakota Sun Dance of 1883." MS no. 1394a, National Anthropological Archives, Smithsonian Institution.

Zimmerly, David W. 1968. "When the People Gather: Notes on Teton Dakota Sun Dancing." Indian Health Service, *Pine Ridge Research Bulletin*, no. 6.

THE VISION QUEST

Albers, Patricia, and Seymour Parker. 1971. "The Plains Vision Experience: A Study of Power and Privilege." *Southwestern Journal of Anthropology* 27, no. 3: 203–33.

Benedict, Ruth F. 1922. "The Vision in Plains Culture." *American Anthropologist* 24, no. 1: 1–23.

Blumensohn, Jules. 1933. "The Fast among North American Indians." *American Anthropologist* 35, no. 3: 451–469.

DeMallie, Raymond J. 1984. "John G. Neihardt's Lakota Legacy." In *A Sender of Words: Essays in Memory of John G Neihardt*, ed. Vine Deloria Jr. Chicago and Salt Lake City: Howe Bros.

Howard, James H. 1951. "Two Dakota Dream Headdresses." W. H. Over Museum, University of South Dakota, *Museum News* 12, no. 4: 1–3.

Powers, William K. 1982. *Yuwipi: Vision and Experience in Oglala Ritual*. Lincoln: University of Nebraska Press.

Steltenkamp, Michael F. 1982. *The Sacred Vision: Native American Religion and Its Practice Today*. New York: Paulist Press.

———. 1993. *Black Elk: Holy Man of the Oglala*. Norman: University of Oklahoma Press.

Stoltzman, William, S.J. 1986. *The Pipe and Christ*. Chamberlain SD: Tipi Press.

YUWÍPI

Feraca, Stephen E. 1961. "The Yuwipi Cult of the Oglala and Sicangu Teton Sioux." *Plains Anthropologist* 6, no. 13: 155–63.

Grobsmith, Elizabeth S. 1974. "Wakunza: Uses of Yuwipi Medicine Power in Contemporary Teton Dakota Culture." *Plains Anthropologist* 19: 129–33.

Hurt, Wesley R. 1960a. "A Yuwipi Ceremony at Pine Ridge." *Plains Anthropologist* 5, no. 10: 48–52.

———, with James H. Howard. 1952. "A Dakota Conjuring Ceremony." *Southwestern Journal of Anthropology* 8: 286–96.

Kemnitzer, Luis S. 1970. "Cultural Provenience of Artifacts Used in Yuwipi, A Modern Teton Dakota Healing Ritual." *Ethnos* 35: 40–75.

———. 1975. "A 'Grammar Discovery Procedure' for the Study of a Dakota Healing

Ritual." In *Linguistics and Anthropology: In Honor of C. F. Voegelin*, ed. M. Dale Kinkade, Kenneth L. Hale, and Oswald Werner. Lisse, Netherlands: Peter de Ridder Press. 405–22.

————. 1976. "Structure, Content and Cultural Meaning of Yuwipi: A Modern Lakota Healing Ritual." *American Ethnologist* 3: 261–80.

Powers, William K. 1986. *Sacred Language: The Nature of Supernatural Discourse in Lakota*. Norman: University of Oklahoma Press.

OTHER CEREMONIES AND PRACTICES

Corum, Charles Ronald. 1975. "A Teton Tipi Cover Depiction of the Sacred Pipe Myth." *South Dakota History* 5, no. 3: 229–44.

Dorsey, George A. 1906. "Legend of the Teton Sioux Medicine Pipe." *Journal of American Folklore* 19: 326–29.

Feraca, Stephen E. 1962. "The Teton Sioux Eagle Medicine Cult." *American Indian Tradition* 51, no. 5–8: 195–96.

Fletcher, Alice C. 1884. "The White Buffalo Festival of the Uncpapas." Report of the Peabody Museum of American Archaeology and Ethnology, no. 16. Salem MA: Salem Press. 260–78.

Fugle, Eugene. 1966. "The Nature and Function of the Lakota Night Cults." W. H Over Museum, University of South Dakota, *Museum News* 27: 1–38.

Howard, James H. 1952. "A Yanktonai Dakota Mide Bundle." *North Dakota History* 192: 132–39.

————. 1954. "The Dakota Heyoka Cult." *The Scientific Monthly* 78, no. 4: 254–58.

————. 1955. "The Tree Dweller Cults of the Dakota." *Journal of American Folklore* 68, no. 268: 169–74.

————. 1961. "A Note on the Dakota Water Drinking Society." *American Indian Tradition* 7, no. 3: 96.

Lewis, Thomas. 1974. "The Heyoka Cult in Historical and Contemporary Oglala Sioux Society." *Anthropos* 69: 1–32.

Pond, Gideon H. 1854. "Power and Influence of Dakota Medicine Men." In *Information Respecting the History, Conditions and Prospects of the Indian Tribes of the United States*, ed. Henry Schoolcraft. Vol. 4. 641–51.

Smith, John L. 1967. "A Short History of the Sacred Calf Pipe of the Teton Sioux." W. H. Over Museum, University of South Dakota, *Museum News* 28: 1–37.

Thomas, Sidney J. 1941. "A Sioux Medicine Bundle." *American Anthropologist* 43: 605–9.

Wissler, Clark. 1905. "The Whirlwind and the Elk in the Mythology of the Dakota." *Journal of American Folklore* 18: 257–68.

———. 1916. *General Discussion of Shamanistic and Dancing Societies.* Anthropological Papers, vol. 11, pt. 12. American Museum of Natural History. New York: The Trustees. 853–76.

Zimmerly, David. 1969. "On Being an Ascetic: Personal Document of a Sioux Medicine Man." Indian Health Service, *Pine Ridge Research Bulletin,* no. 10: 46–71.

PEYOTISM

Howard, James H. 1957. "The Mescal Bean Cult of the Central and Southern Plains: An Ancestor of the Peyote Cult?" *American Anthropologist* 59, no. 1: 75–87.

———. 1962. "Peyote Jokes." *Journal of American Folklore* 75: 10–14.

———. 1967. "Half Moon Way: The Peyote Ritual of Chief White Bear." W. H. Over Museum, University of South Dakota, *Museum News* 29: 1–24.

Hurt, Wesley R. 1960b. "Factors in the Persistence of Peyote in the Northern Plains." *Plains Anthropologist* 5, no. 9: 16–27.

La Barre, Weston. 1938. *The Peyote Cult.* Yale University Publications in Anthropology, no. 19. New Haven: Yale University Press.

Steinmetz, Paul B., S.J. 1990. "Shamanic Images in Peyote Visions." In *Religion in Native North America,* ed. Christopher Vecsey. Moscow: University of Idaho Press.

HERBALISM

Gilmore, Melvin R. 1919. *Uses of Plants by the Indians of the Missouri River Region.* Bureau of American Ethnology, Smithsonian Institution, annual report 33. Reprints, Lincoln: University of Nebraska Press, 1977, 1991.

Howard, James H. 1953. "Notes on Two Dakota Holy Dance Medicines and Their Uses." *American Anthropologist* 55, no. 4: 608–9.

Lewis, Thomas H. 1990. *The Medicine Men: Oglala Sioux Ceremony and Healing.* Lincoln: University of Nebraska Press.

Rogers, Dilwyn J. 1980a. *Lakota Names and Traditional Uses of Native Plants.* St. Francis sd: Rosebud Educational Society.

———. 1980b. *Edible, Medicinal, Useful and Poisonous Wild Plants of the Northern Great Plains–South Dakota Region.* St. Francis sd: Buechel Museum.

Vogel, Virgil J. 1970. *American Indian Medicine.* Norman: University of Oklahoma Press.